Origami - The Japanese Art of Paper Folding

I0488666

Isao Honda

CONTENTS

Introduction

Like tea and gunpowder, paper was introduced to Western civilization from the East; the Chinese invented it 18 centuries ago. Also from China and Japan came a form of art in paper, Origami (literally "folding paper"). Origami has been known to the Chinese and Japanese about as long as paper itself.

Origami calls for precision and imagination. If you flip through the pages of this book, you will find a great variety of familiar things conceived with imagination, style, and often a good deal of humor. Anyone can do this—it has been the special province of Oriental children for centuries—by closely following the step-by-step directions. The result is the gradual yet magical materialization of a solid object which delights a child. It is not surprising that Origami is taught in many South American schools. Patience, control, and perseverance in following all directions closely— which are the requisites of Origami—are part of the mental discipline necessary for a child's growth into maturity.

But adults enjoy Origami just as much. It satisfies the same impulse which, for instance, prompts Winston Churchill to paint; it is an absorbing, creative, and entertaining hobby. Such different men as Shelley and Houdini were ardent paper-folders. Anyone who has completed this book can then go on to invent his own designs.

This is the ideal book on Origami: the directions are clear; they are fully illustrated.

LILLIAN OPPENHEIMER
Founder of the Origami Center New York

General directions

The right side of the paper is shown in color in all the diagrams. Where there are ordinary dotted lines, fold over. This is called a valley fold. Along dotted lines marked with a P, fold under. This is called a peak fold. Cut with scissors along lines marked C.

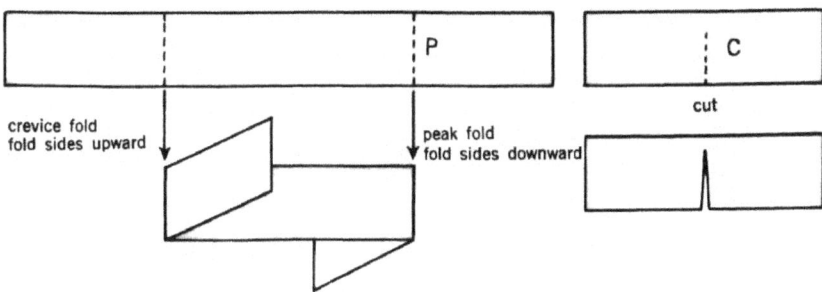

In making the more advanced patterns it often helps to prepare the sheet by first creasing it in the following manner: A) Place the square sheet on a table, fold upper edge over lower edge, and crease. We shall call this a middle crease. Open the sheet and repeat the same operation with the other two edges of the square. B) Place the square sheet open in front of you with one corner up, like a diamond. Bring point to point. We shall call this a diaper crease. Open the sheet again and repeat the same operation with the other two points. Your sheet is now creased with four lines all meeting in the center.

When creasing or folding always make sure that edges and points meet exactly.

Most people have less difficulty in folding when they keep the paper in the same position as the diagrams in the book.

Most of the figures here are made with a square piece of paper, but two require a piece cut into an equilateral triangle (a triangle with equal sides). This can be done easily with the aid of a draftsman's ready-made 60° triangle.

Cup

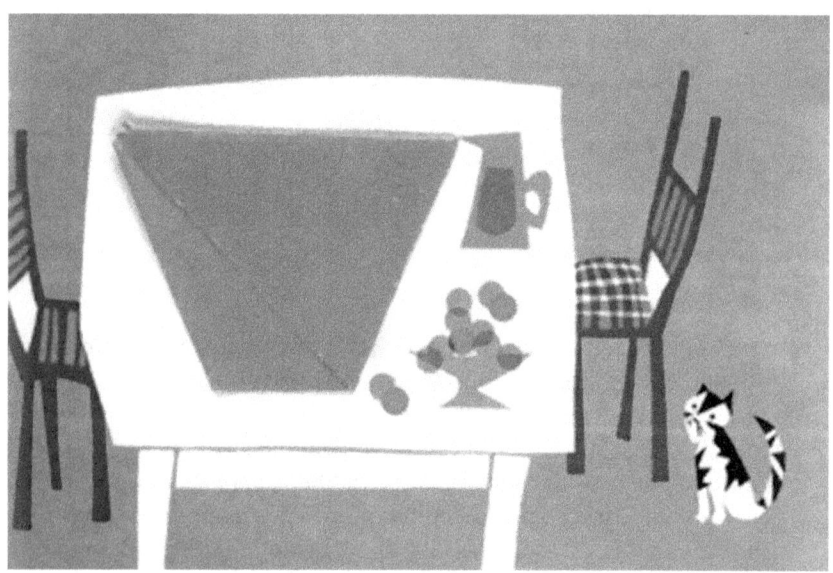

Use a square piece of paper. First make a diaper fold as shown in 1. Then in Step 1, fold so that Line A is parallel to Line B, a valley fold.

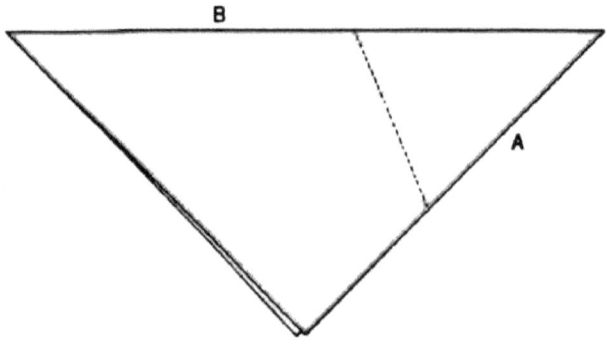

Now for Step 2, fold the other end under in the same way with a peak fold. In Step 3, tuck one bottom flap into each side. If you make the cup out of strong paper, it will hold water.

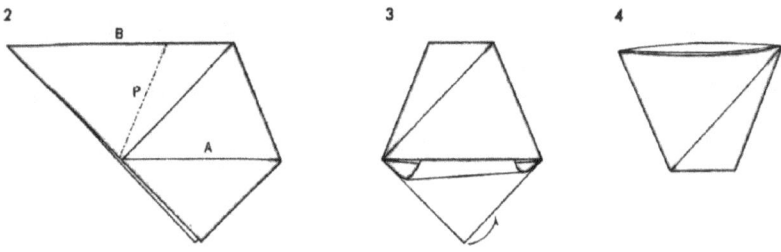

Swan

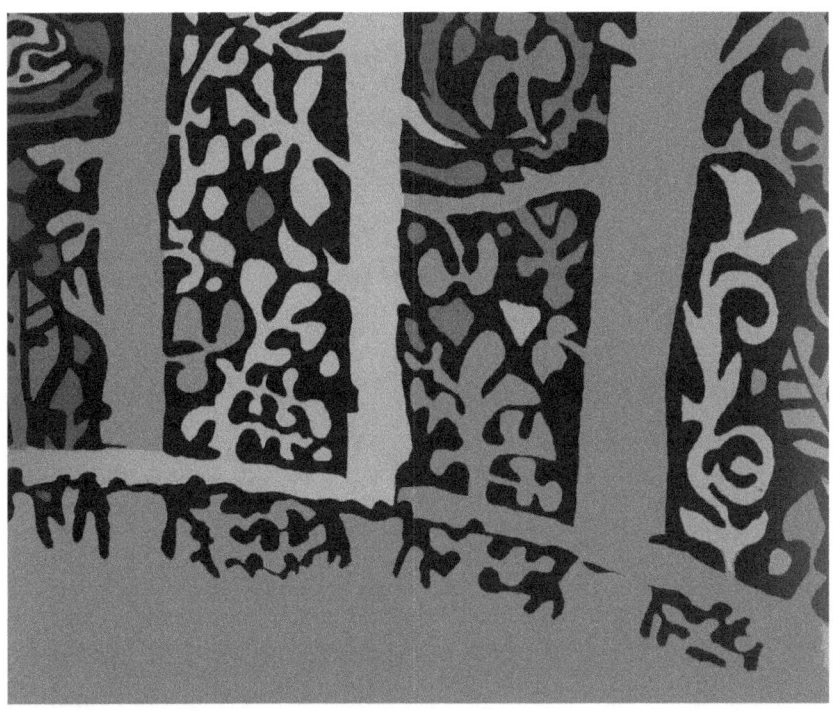

It is easier to fold this if you put the paper down flat on a table. First make a diaper crease (see General Directions). This makes a center line to guide you through the other steps.

In Step 1, fold the top and bottom corners in so that the sides fall on the center line. Then in Step 2, fold down the center line, and in Step 3, fold both sides outward and over.

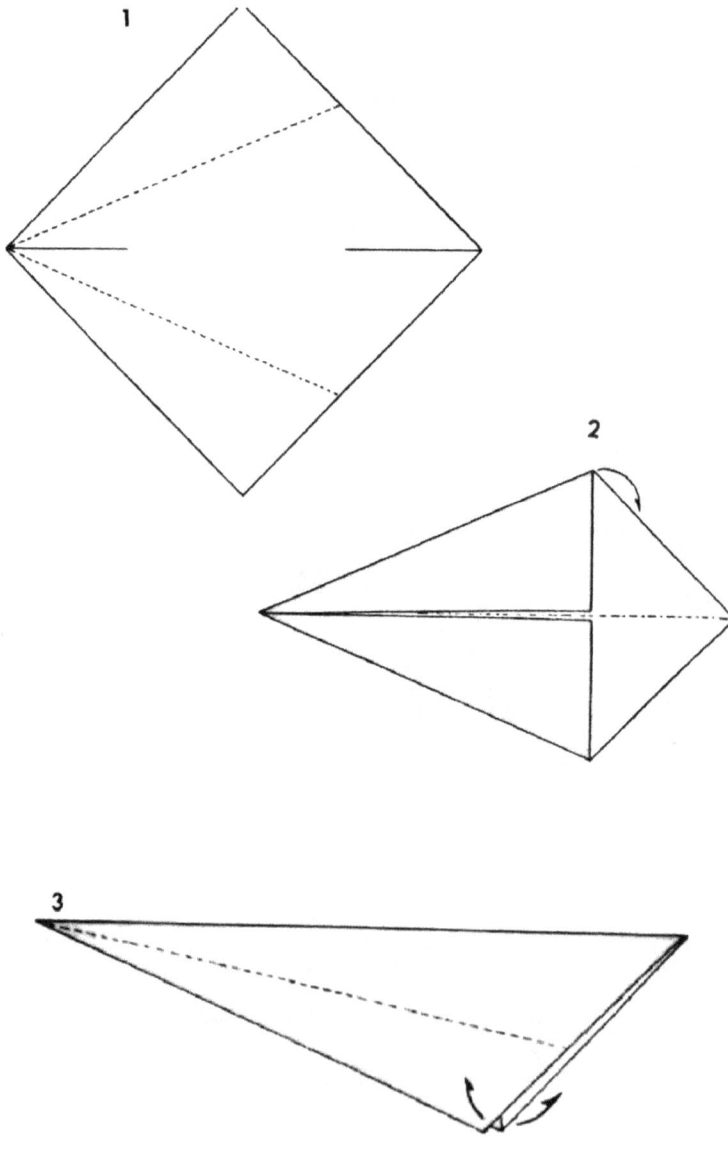

In Step 4, the paper must be turned inside out when it is folded. If you have trouble, detach and examine the swan in the picture. Step 5 includes the folds for the head and tail. Make the head as shown in the enlargement. Heads for other birds and animals are made in much the same way. To make the tail, first fold down along the P-line and then up along the other line. In both cases turn the paper outside in when folding.

4

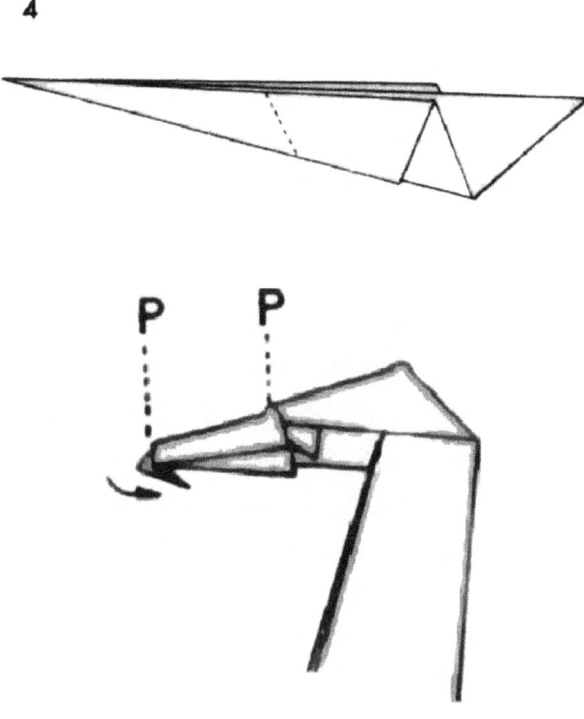

5

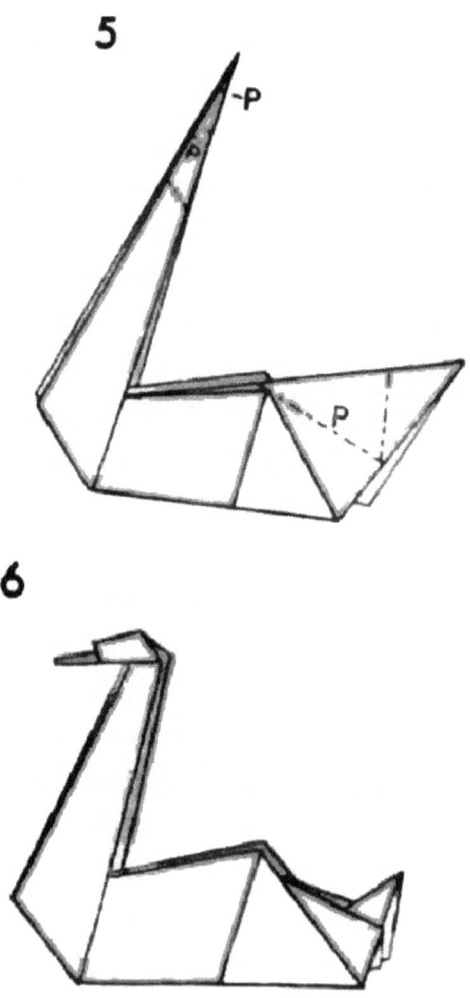

6

Missile

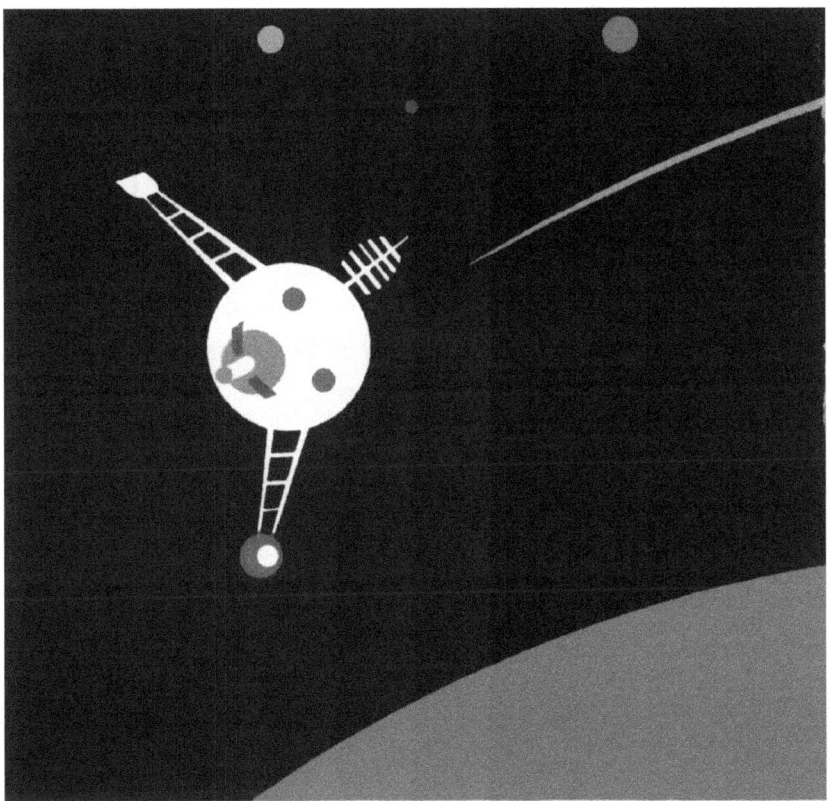

Start with a piece of notebook or tablet paper. In Step 1, fold the top corners to the middle, and in Step 2, fold this end over so that the point comes almost to the edge of the other end. In Step 3, fold the top corners in so that the edges meet along the center.

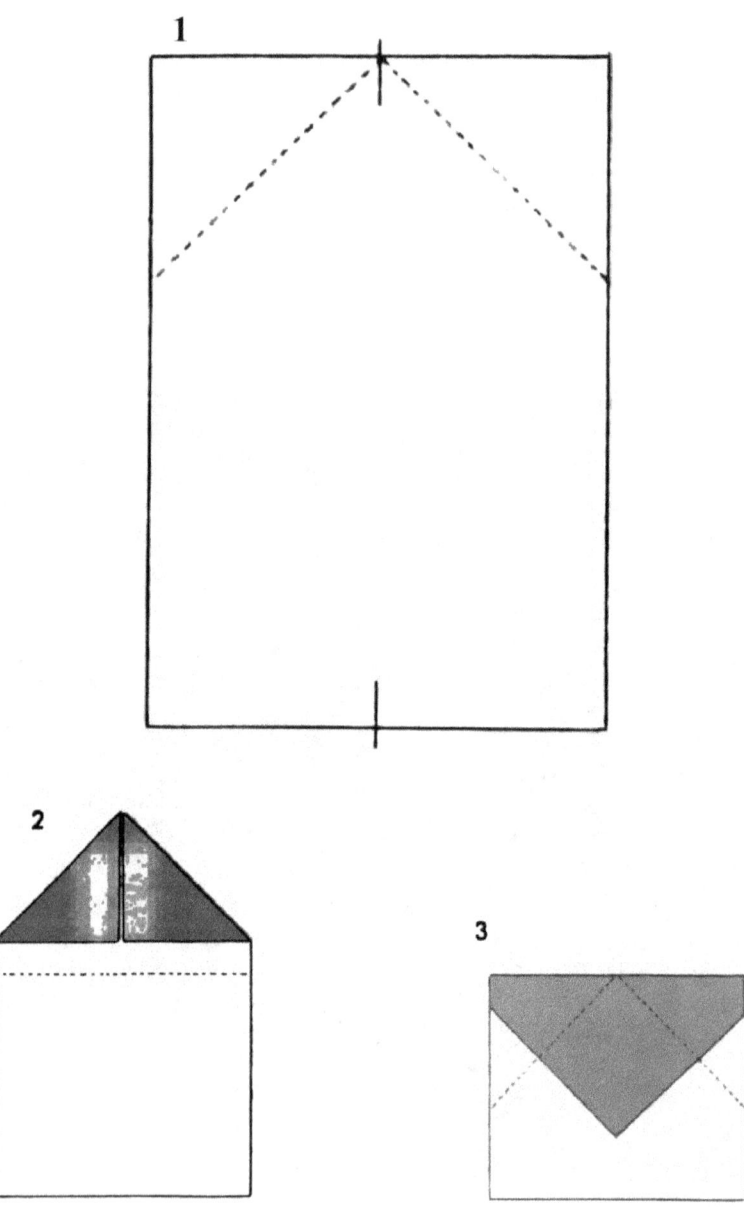

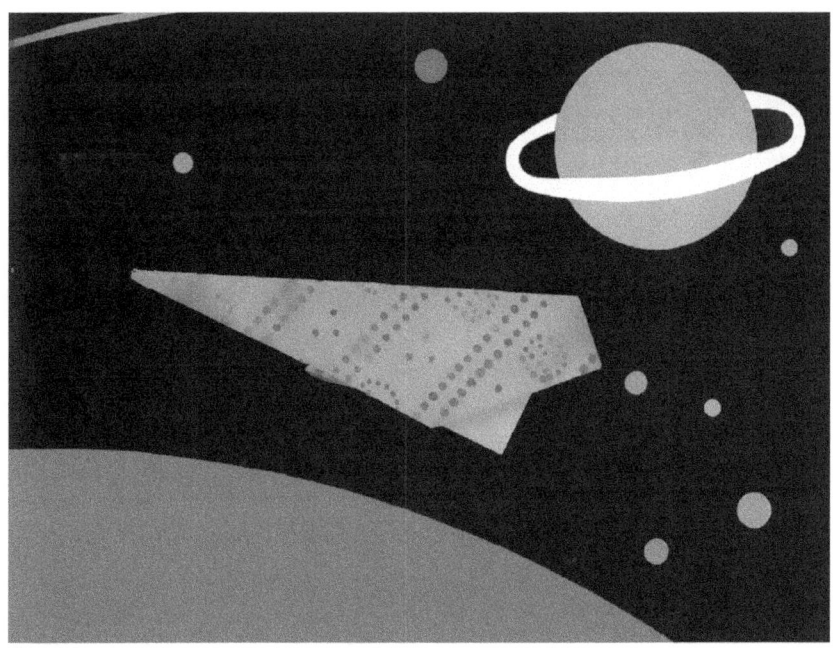

In Step 4, first fold the tip in the middle back, and then fold down the center. In Step 5, fold the sides down to make the wings. After creasing the wings down, spread them out, as in 7. The missile will fly better if you do not throw it too hard.

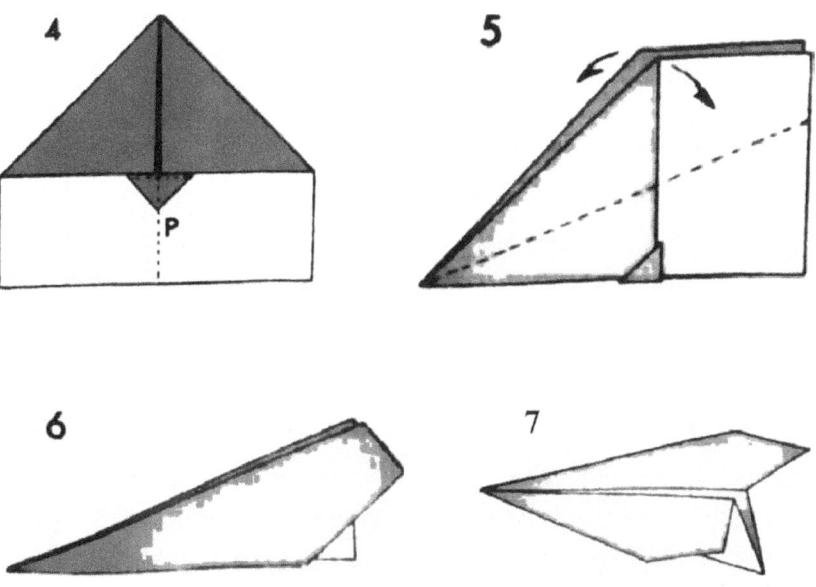

8

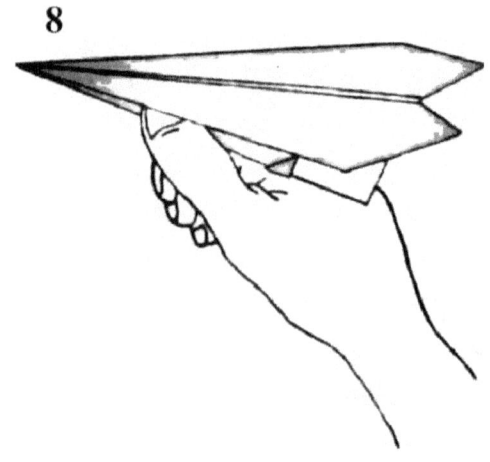

Pin-wheel

In Step 1, fold the two corners over and in along the dotted lines, and in Step 2 fold the other two corners in the same way, but under instead of over. Then in Steps 3 and 4, repeat the first two steps on the smaller squares.

1

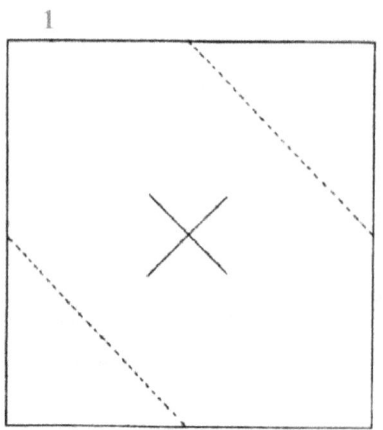

2

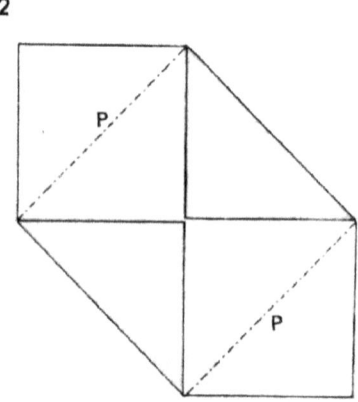

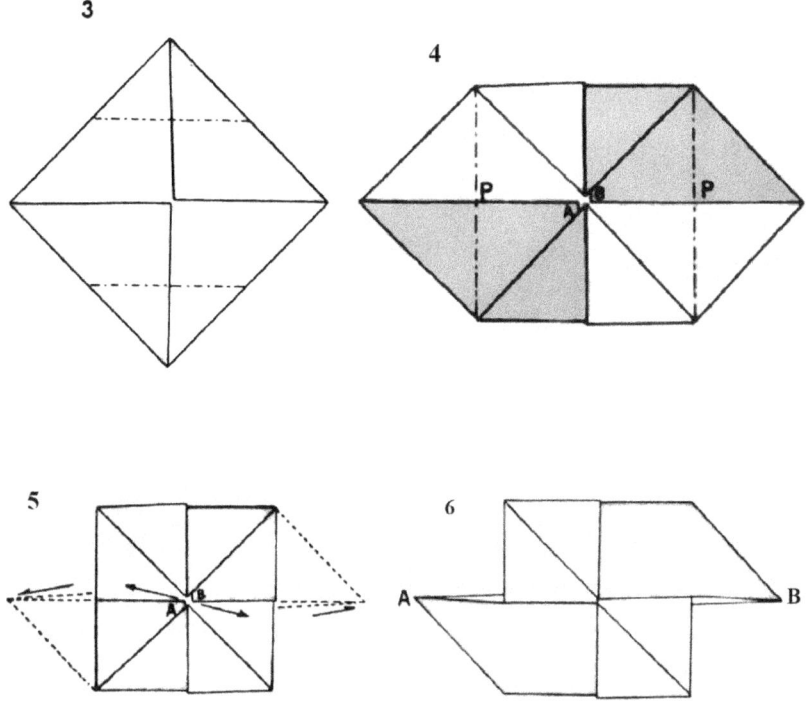

In Step 5, pull Points A and B out to make the shape shown in 6. Then turn over, and in Step 7, pull Points C and D out in the same way. To finish make a hole in the center and mount the pin-wheel on a stick or a knitting needle.

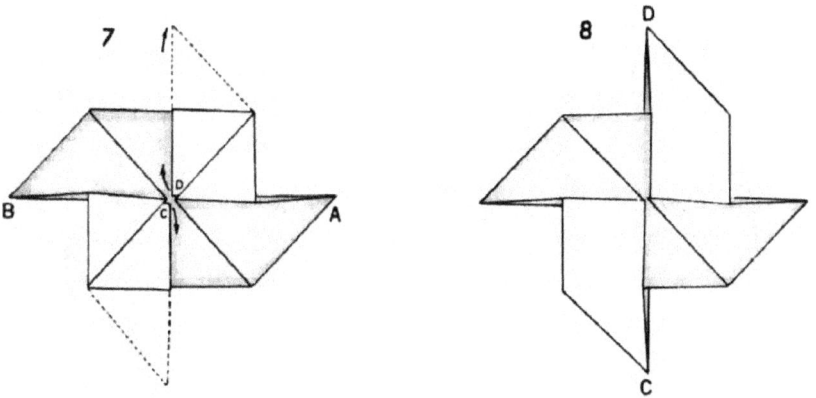

9

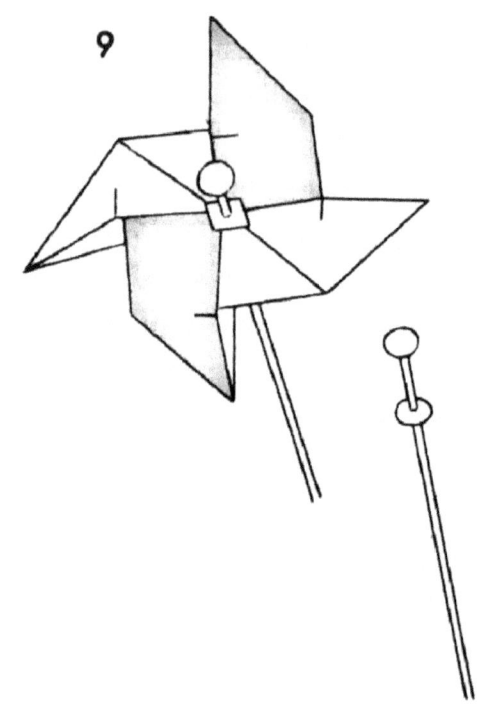

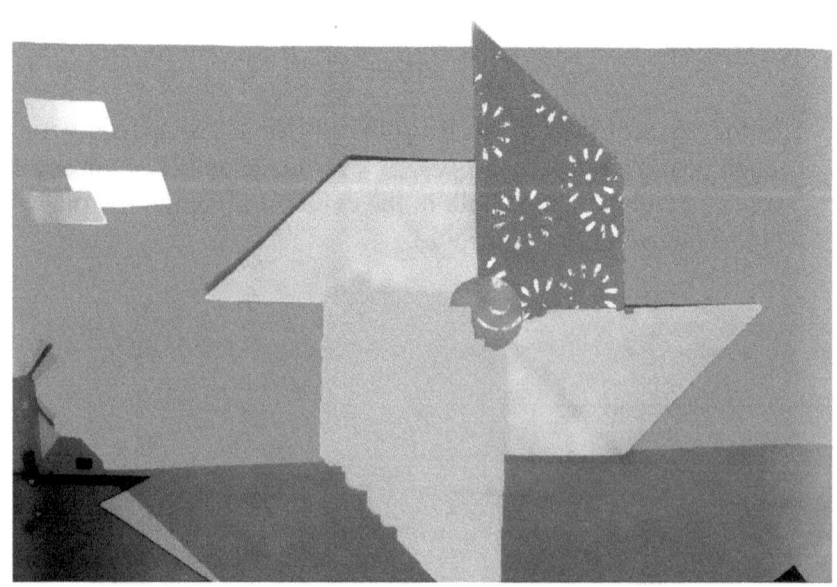

Folding box

Start with a piece of paper that is longer than it is wide. If you use the paper in the back of this book, cut off one quarter of its width.

In Step 1, fold the outside edges in toward the middle, and in Step 2, make a peak fold along the dotted line (in other words, fold the top half under).

Step 3 is a little easier if you crease along Lines 1 and 2 before beginning. After doing this, open and lift the top layer at Points A and B and fold it over at the same time. Points A and B should come out at the top corners, and there will be a fold along Line 3 as shown in Diagram 4. In Step 4, repeat Step 3 on the other side.

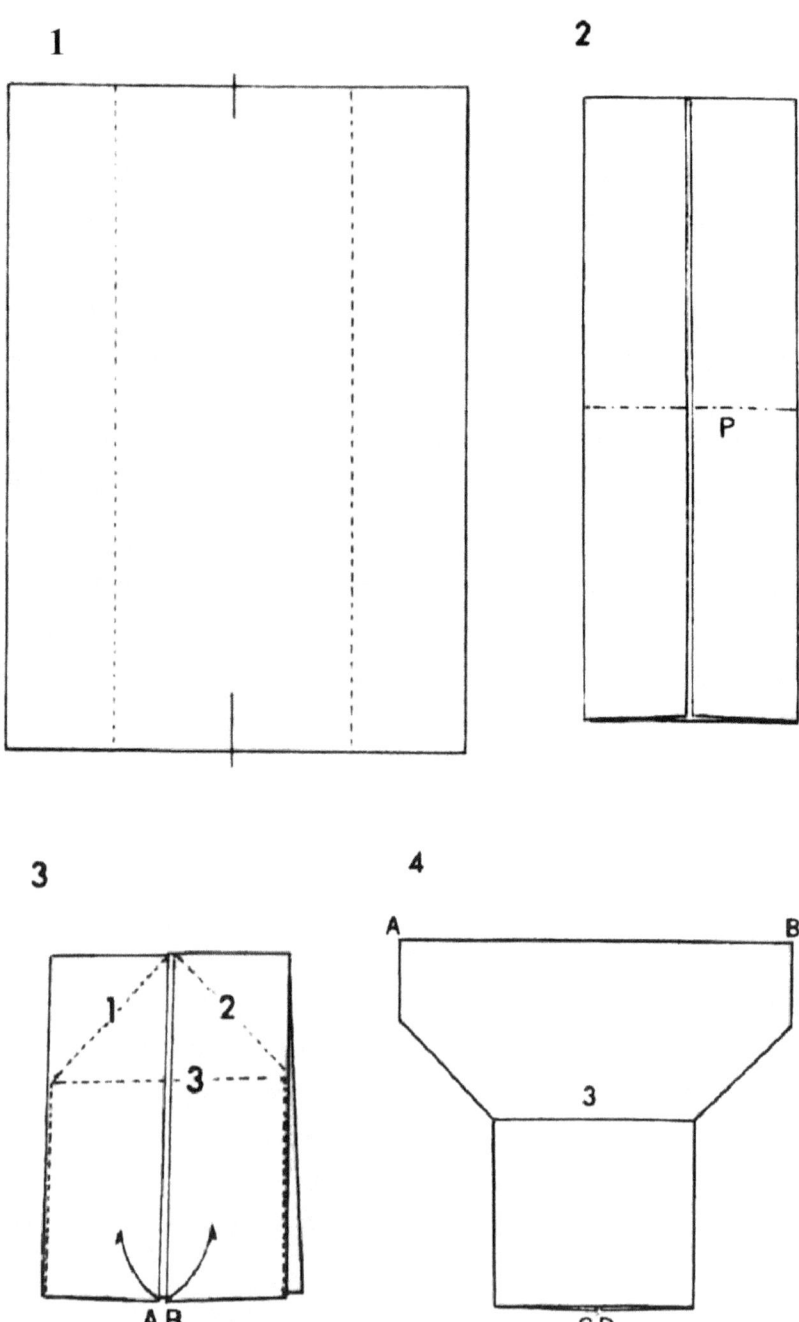

5

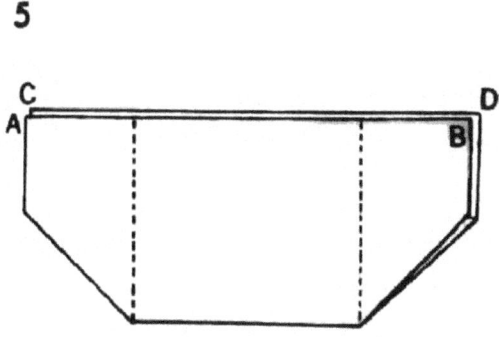

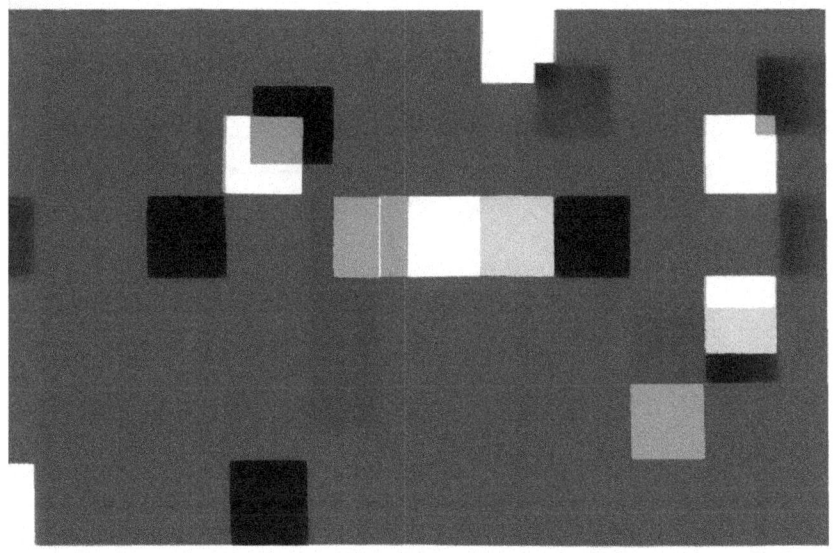

6

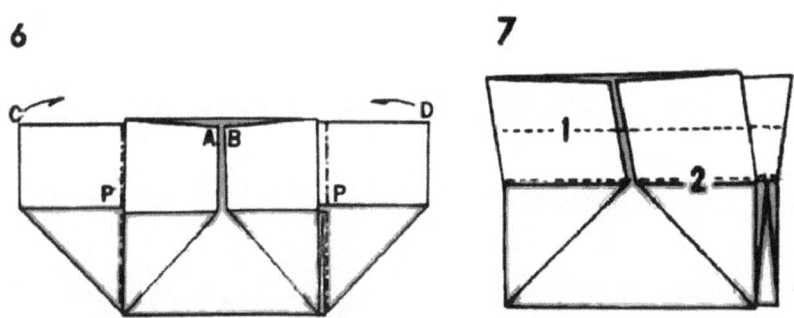

7

8

9

10

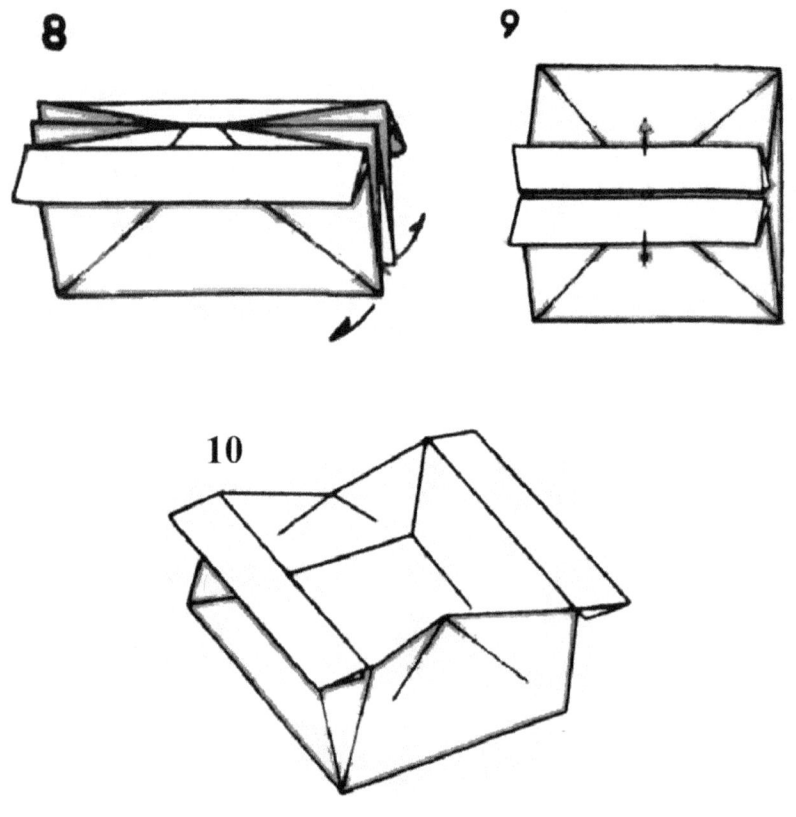

Basic form

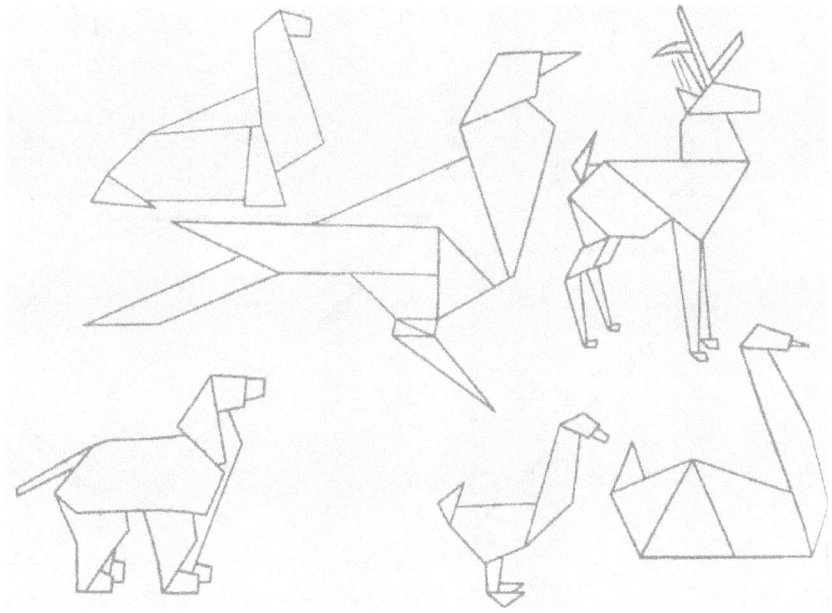

This form Is used In making most origami birds and animals. Prepare the paper as explained in Paragraph 2 of the General Directions.

Start with a diaper fold and in Step 1, fold it again. Then, in Step 2, pick up the top sheet at the point shown by the arrow, and turn it outward and over, bringing Point A to meet Point B, as shown in 3. Now turn the paper over, and in Step 4, repeat Step 2 on the other side. In Step 5, fold the outside bottom layers on both sides over along the dotted lines.

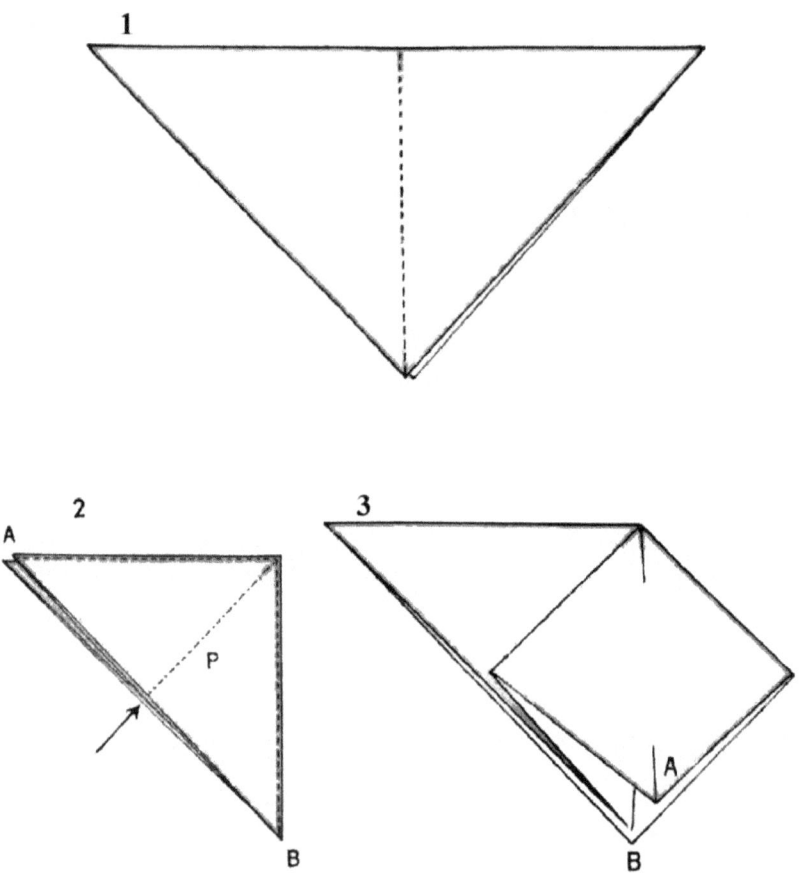

In Step 6 fold the outside edges in so that the sides fall along the center line, and then do the same thing on the other side. The fold for Step 7 is a temporary one. it is included only to make the next step easier.

In Step 8 open the top layer and hold the rest of the lower end with one finger of the left hand over the center line. Then gently bring Point A out to the tip of the peak formed by the dotted lines, turning the outside edges of the paper inward at the same time, as in 9. In doing this you will have to make a fold underneath at the line shown by the arrow in 9. This is the place where the crease was made in Step 7. When the edges have been creased down, you should have a perfect diamond shape on one side. Now do the same thing on the other side. The final two-layer diamond in Diagram 10 is the basic form for making animals and birds.

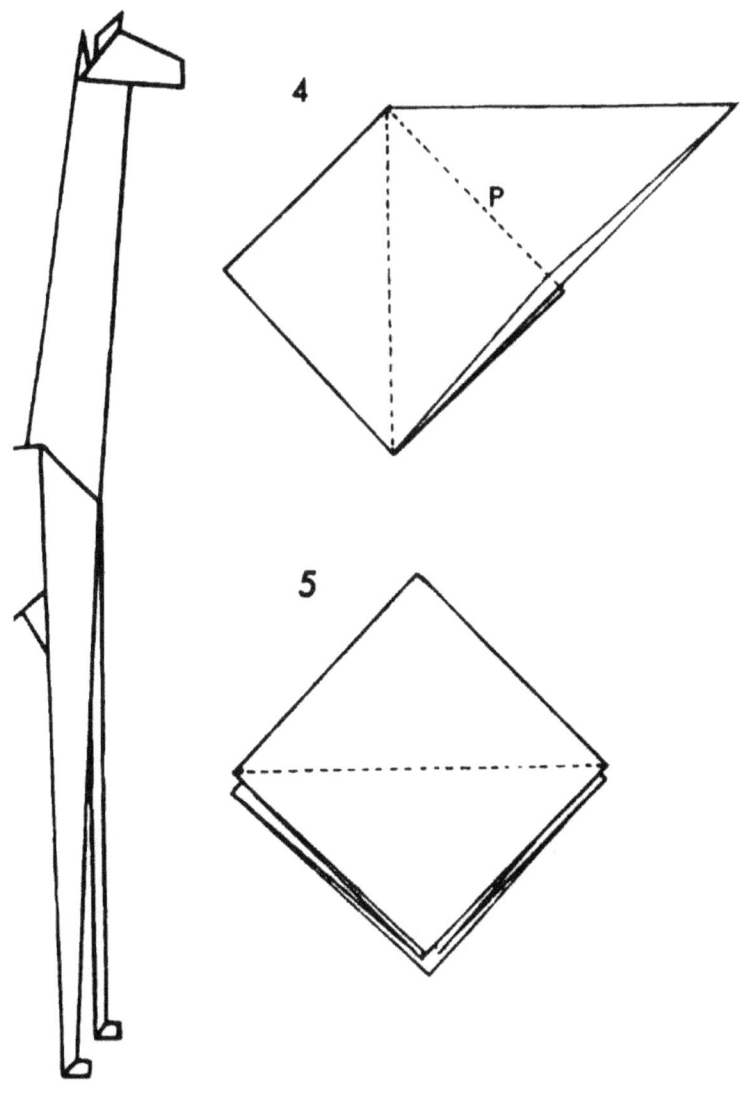

4

P

5

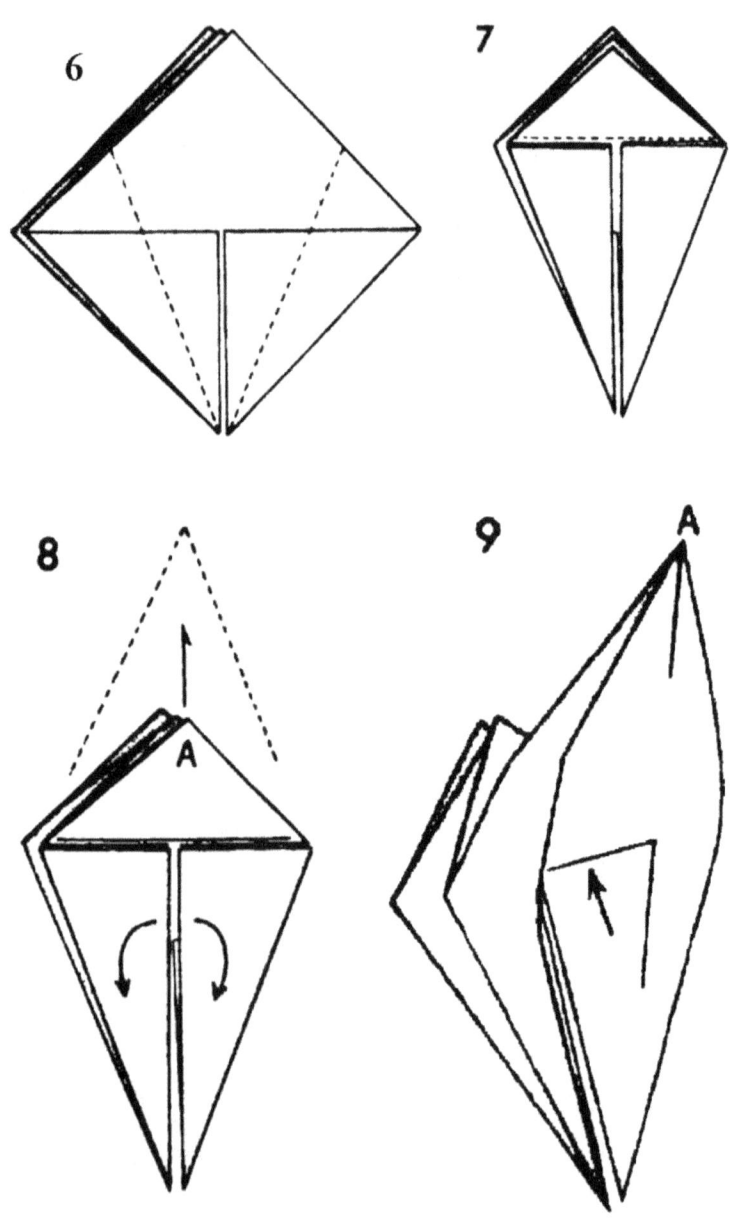

10

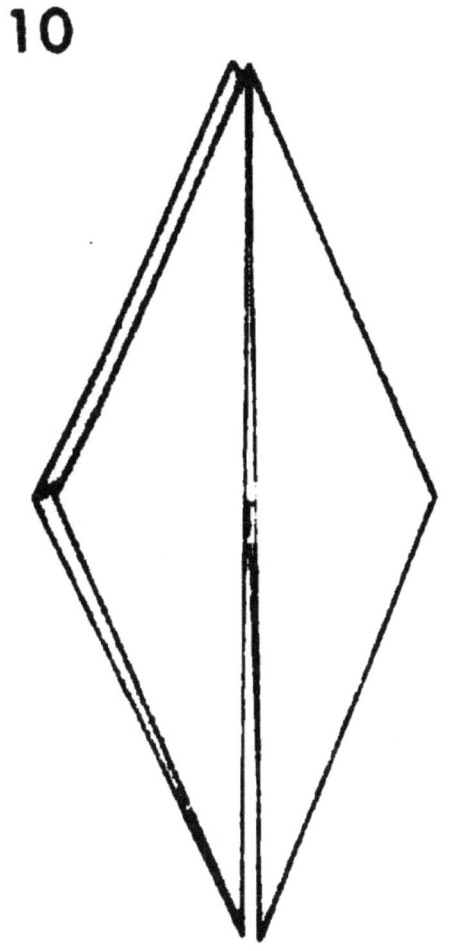

Crane

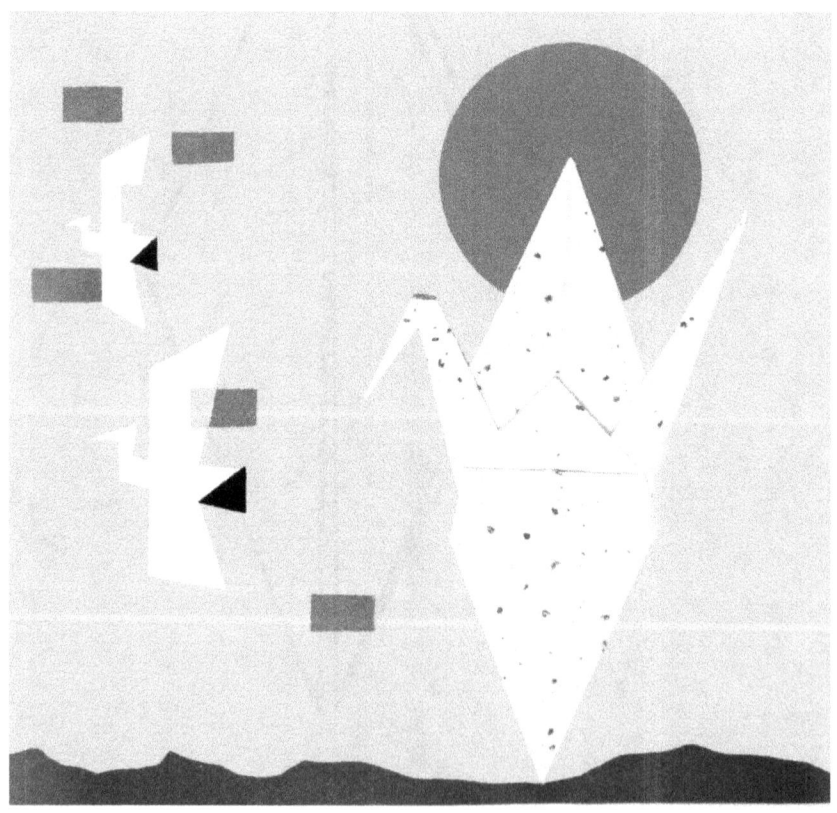

Cranes are considered lucky in Japan, and every Japanese boy and girl can fold paper ones. Once you have learned to make the Basic form, it is easy.

Starting with the basic form, for Step 1, fold the lower outer edges in to the center line, and in Step 2, do the same thing on the other side. Then in Step 3, fold the lower points up, turning them inside out at the same time. This is just the opposite of the way you folded the neck of the Swan. The tips should come out at almost the same level as the top points.

In Step 4, fold the front point down, turning it inside out at the same time. This makes the crane's head. Also, spread out the large flaps to make the wings, and blow air into the hole under the bottom to fill the body.

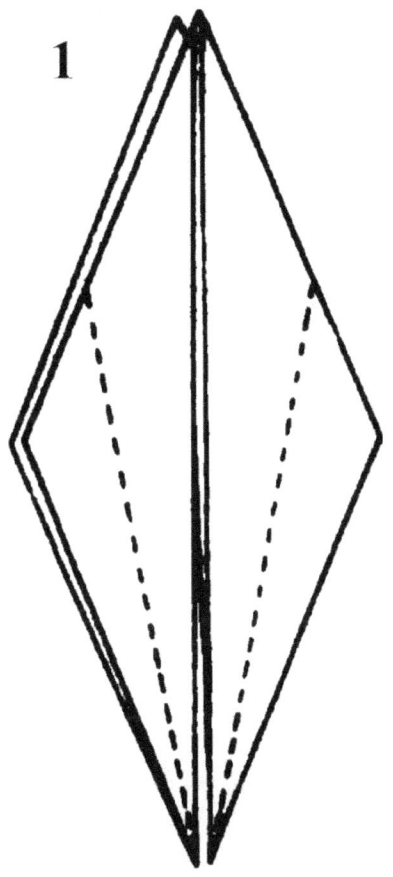

2

3

4

P

5

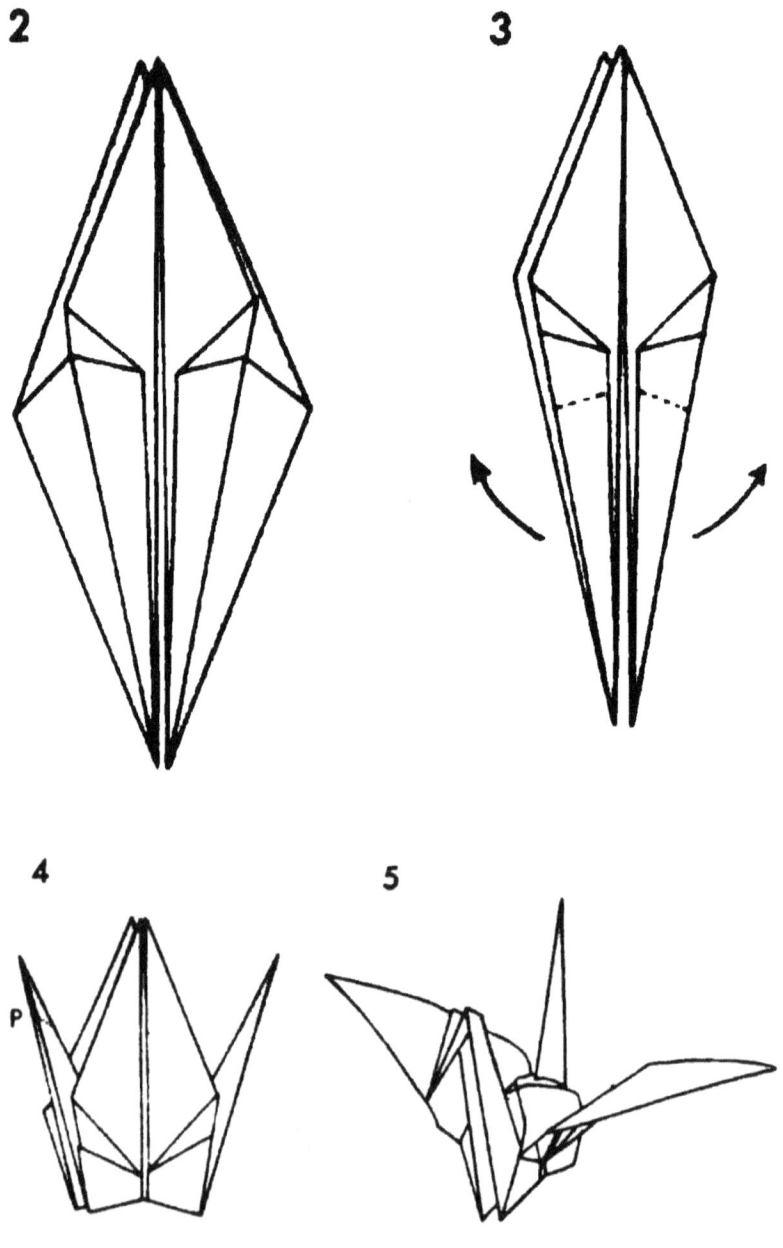

Canary

Start with the basic form. In Step 1, the bottom points are folded up and in. This is like Step 3 for the Crane. In Step 2, fold the top layers of the bottom sections over, and in Step 3, fold both sides of both the bottom sections in toward the middle. This step, as you will see, makes the legs of the bird very thin.

In Step 4, refold the upper parts of the two lower sections. Then in Step 5, fold the back flap down, so that Point B comes to the bottom. In Step 6, fold the diamond down the center. Now we have the canary's body and legs.

In Step 7, fold the front flap back, turning it inside out at the same time. In Step 8, cut along the dotted line, and then on each side fold the lower edge over, pressing down the triangles that appear at the bird's breast. Also fold the top point over, turning it outside in at the same time to make the head.

In Step 9, put the finishing touches on the beak and the legs. These folds are made in the same way as for the beak of the Swan. Also fold the small triangle at the breast in.

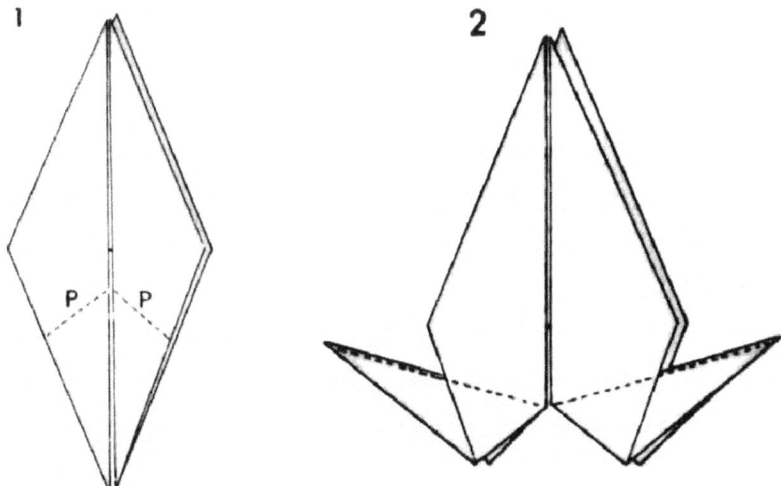

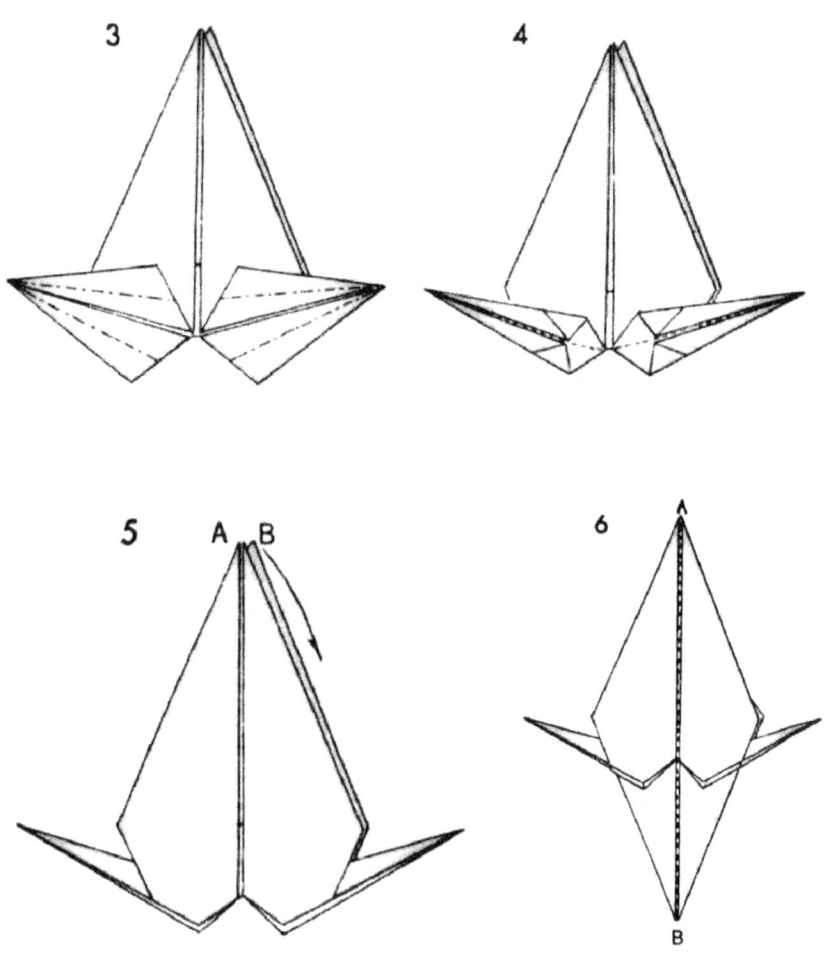

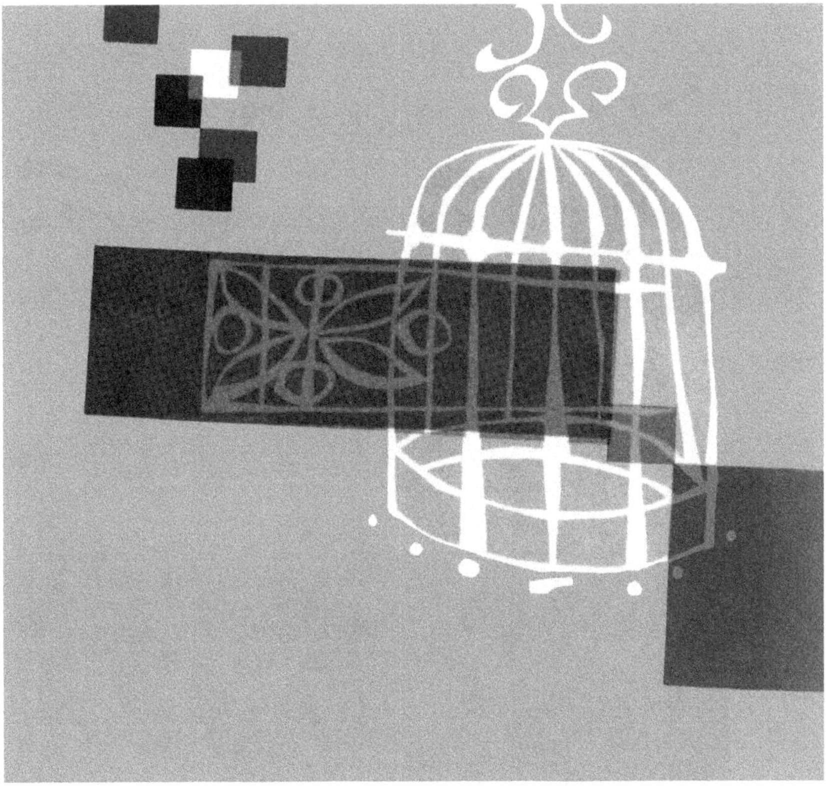

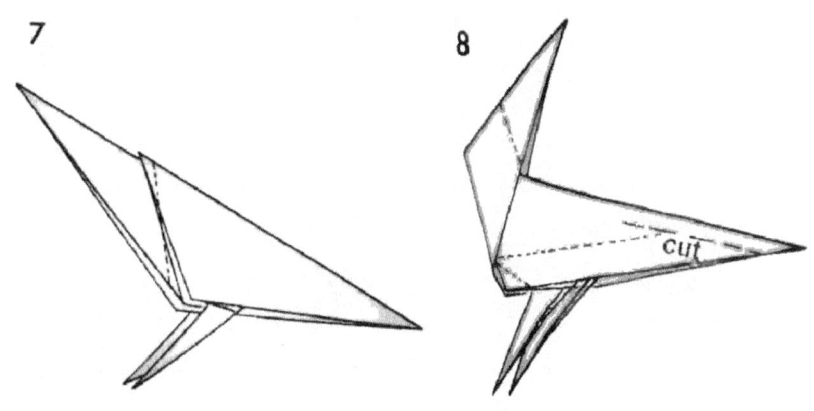

7

8

cut

31

9

10

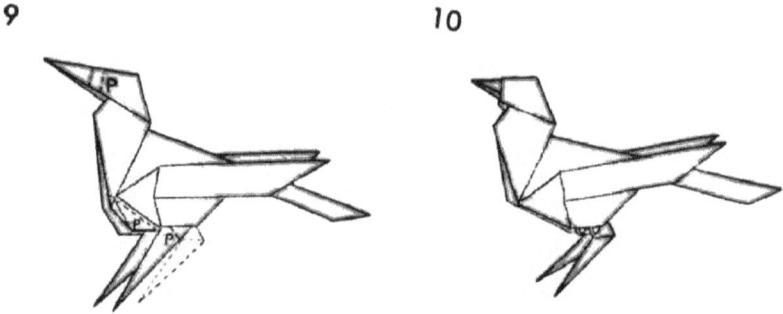

Owl

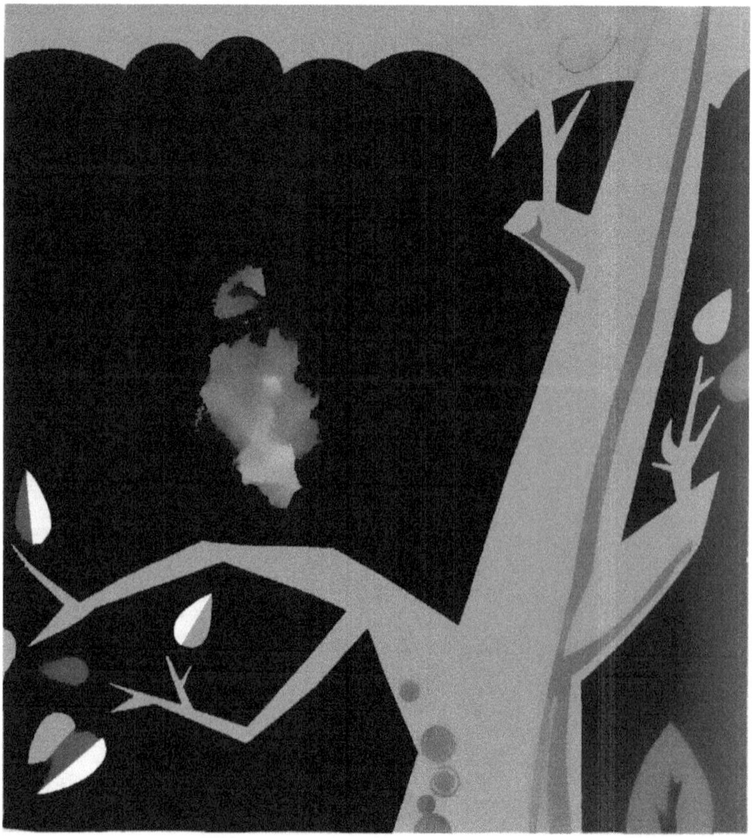

Start with the basic form. In Step 1, fold the top points A and B down to C and D. Then in Step 2, fold the outside corners of the upper layer in, and in Step 3, do the same thing on the other side. Step 4 is a little hard. Holding the figure at the center with the left hand, pul out Point D, and then fold the flap that end with D in such a way as to make the shape shown by the dotted line. Now do the same thing with Point C.

In Step 5, fold back at Line 1, and then forward at both 2 and 3. In Step 6, cut the upper layer along the dotted line. While you have the scissors turn to the back side and cut slits in the back near the top of the head as in Diagram 7 Fold them out to make the ears. Finally fold the bottom points in the front out to make the feet.

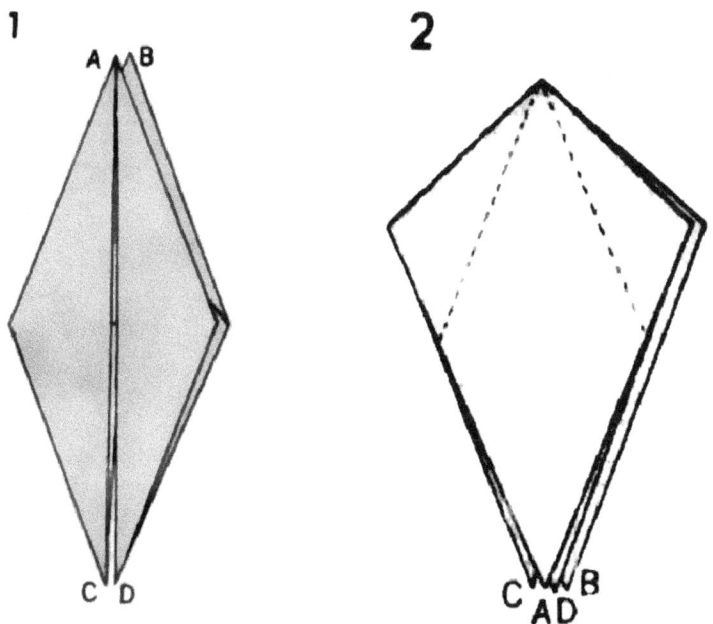

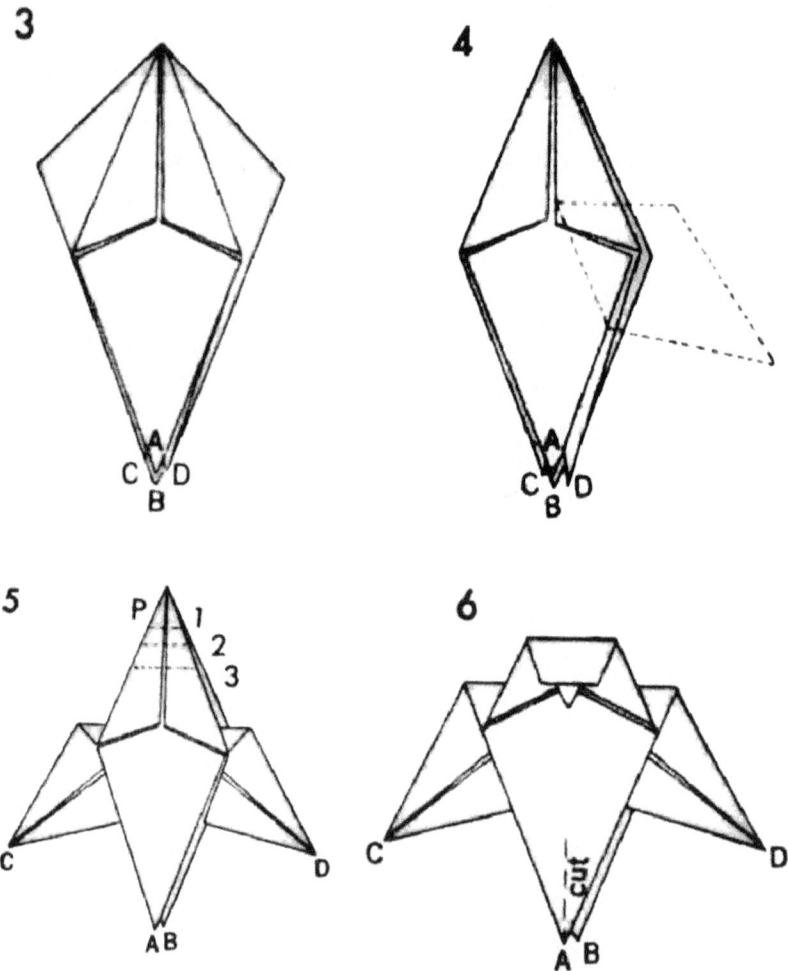

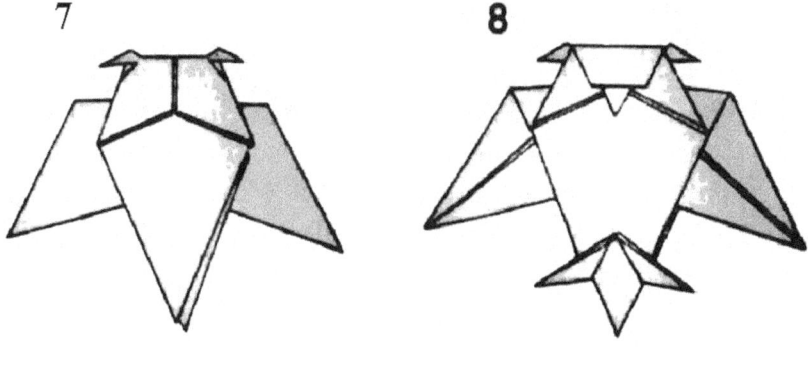

Cat

Head

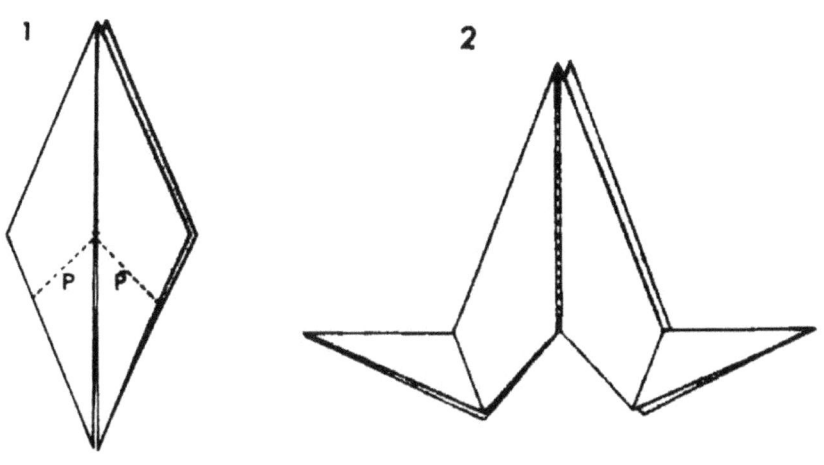

The two parts of the cat are made separately and then pasted together. Both begin with the basic form, and the first step is the same for both. In this first step, the bottom points are not just folded under, but turned inside out and folded at the same time, so that the points come out between the sides of the diamond. In Step 2, for the head, fold down the center line, and in Step 3, fold the front end back, turning it inside out at the same time.

In Steps 4 and 5, bring the top point down toward the front. Then in Step 6, put the finishing touches on the face and legs. In Step 7, make slits on the back side of the head, and turn up the points to make the ears.

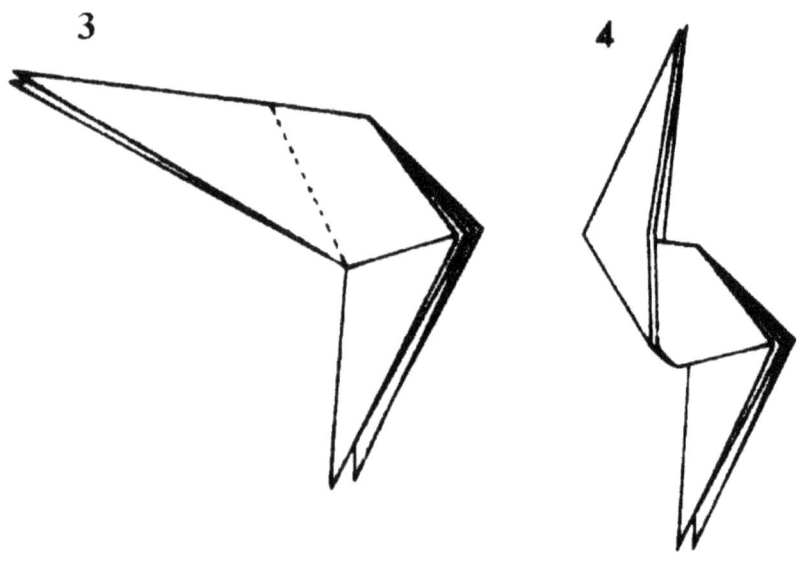

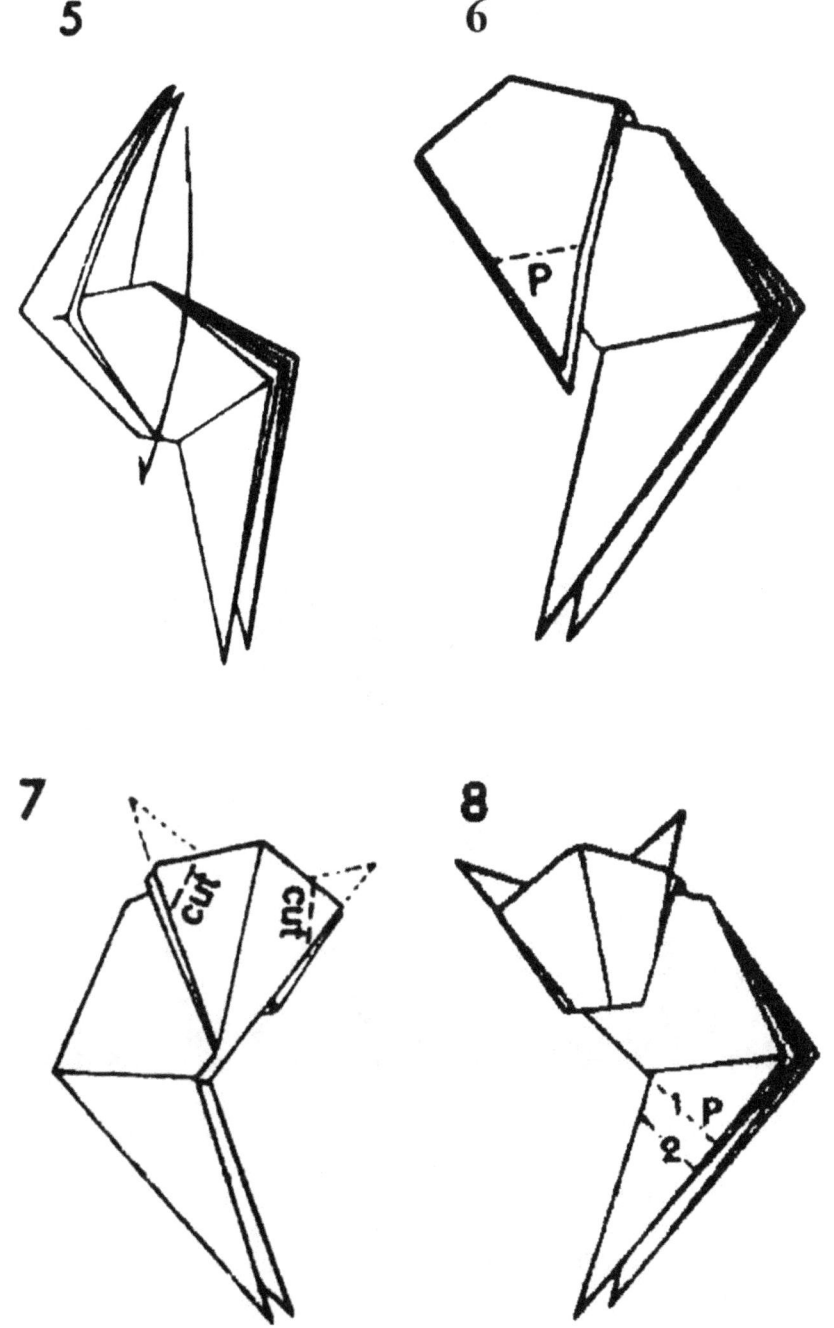

9

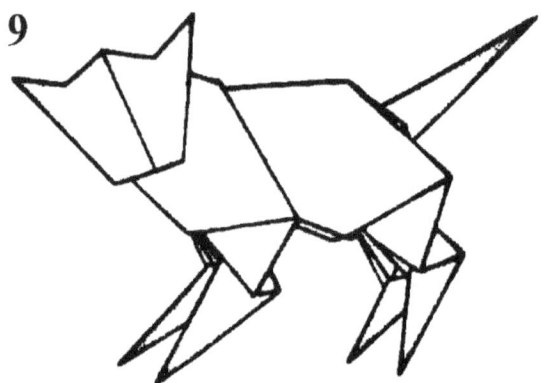

Tail

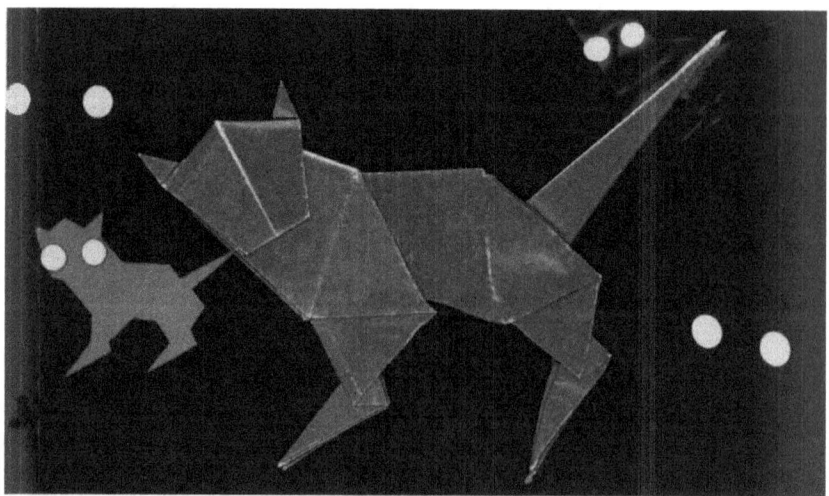

In Step 2, for the tail, fold down the upper flap. Then in Step 3, fold the edges of the lower flap toward the center, and crease down the triangles that appear in the sections where the P-lines are. Also fold down the top point. In Step 4, fold down the center, and in Step 5, make the final folds in the tail and legs. Now paste the head and the tail together.

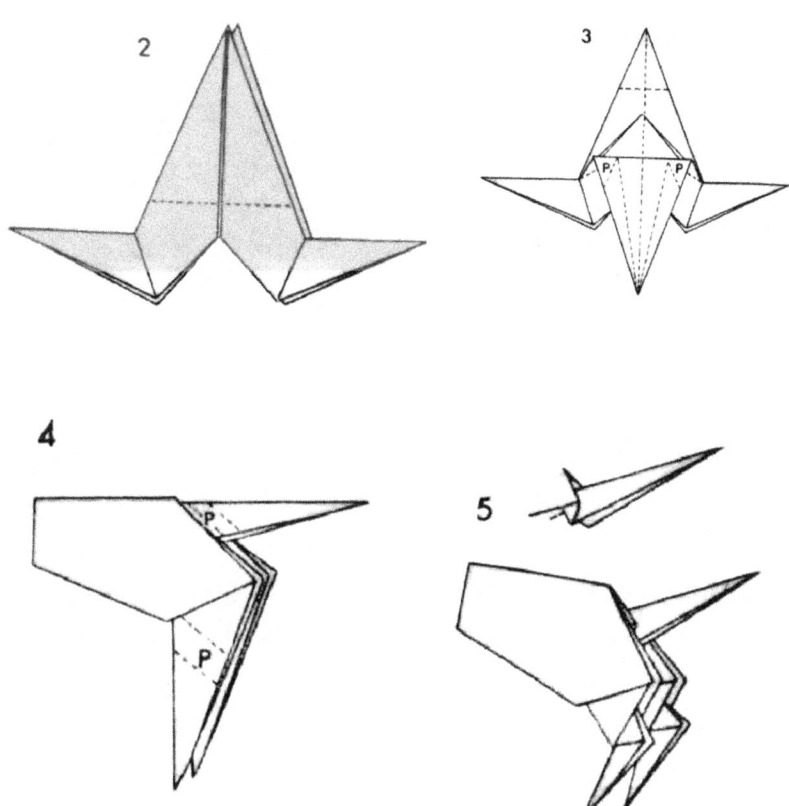

Kangaroo

Head

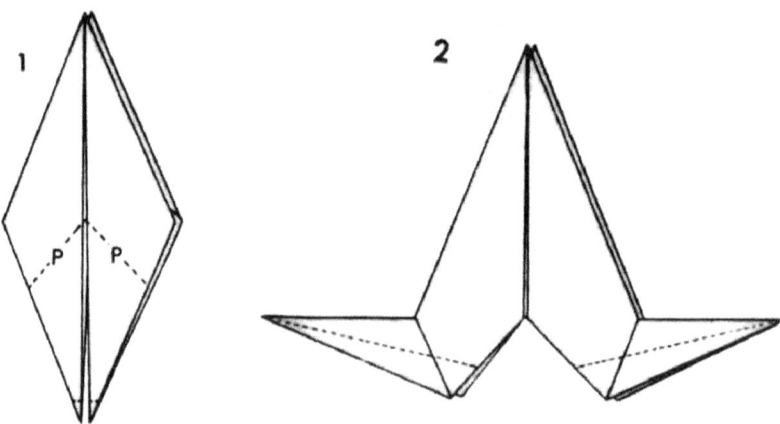

The kangaroo, like the cat, is made in two parts and then pasted together. Both the front and the back begin with the basic form, and Step 1 is the same for both.

In Step 1, fold the lower points of the basic form out, and at the same time turn their edges outside in so that the points come out between the layers of the diamond.

In Step 2, for the head, fold the upper layers over as shown, and then turn the paper over and do the same thing on the other side. In Step 3, fold down the center line.

In Step 4, fold the front part back, turning it outside in at the same time. Then fold the lower two points in exactly the opposite way. That is, turn them inside out when folding under. In Step 5, fold the front layer of the top point forward, again turning it inside out. Also, fold the front tip under to make the mouth the right shape. Then fold the back two points outside in and toward the front.

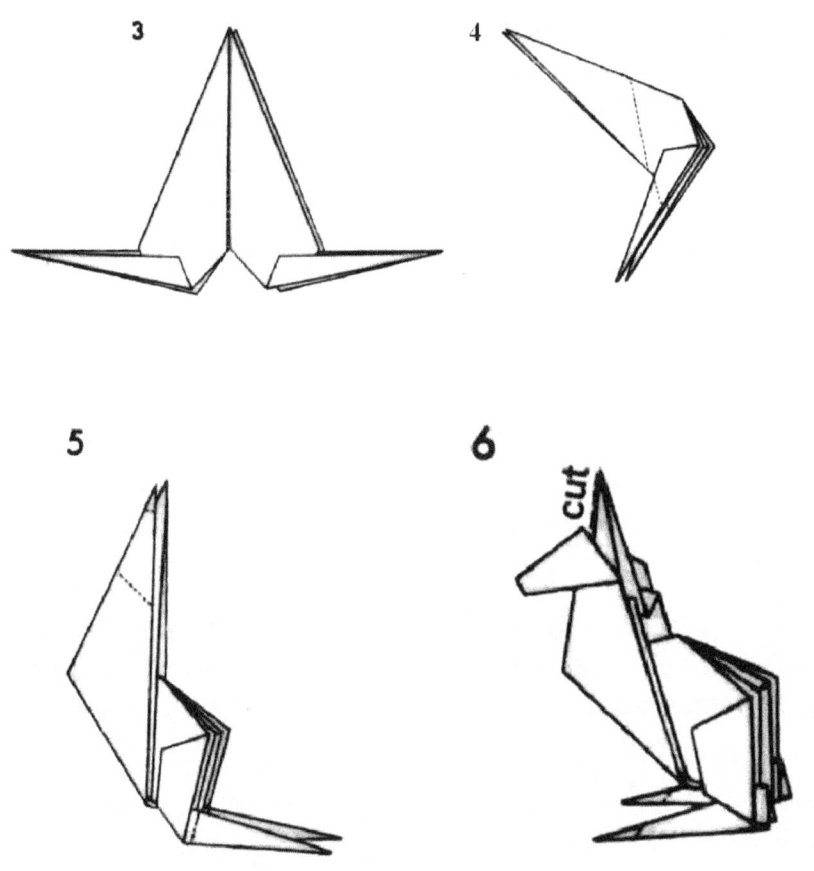

41

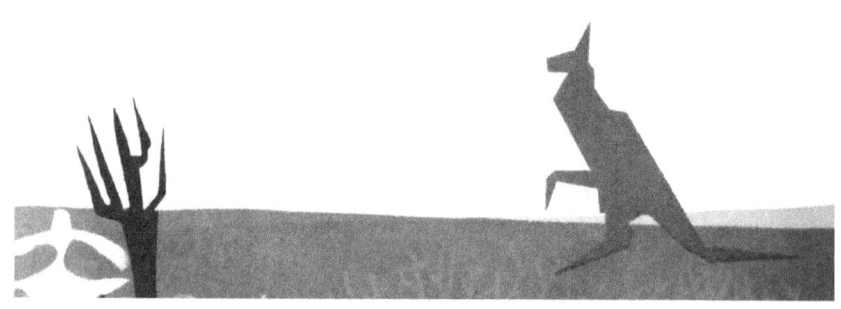

Tail

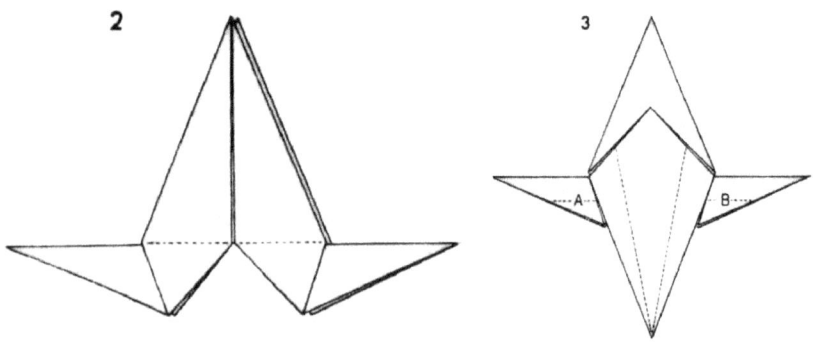

Next fold the tips of the bottom points down to make the paws, and cut down the middle of the top point to separate the ears.

In Step 2 of the back part, fold the top layer of the upper part down, and in Step 3, fold the outside edges of the top layer in to the center. When you do this, the paper under the edges will stand up, and you will have to make the folds on Lines A and B to make it lie down again.

In Step 4, fold the top point toward you. Then fold the lower edges of the outer points over. Now turn the paper over and fold the lower edges on the other side in the same way. Then in Step 5, fold down the center. In Step 6, fold the top point outside in and down, so that it disappears from sight. Then put the finishing touches on the legs in the same fashion as in other animals. Finally, paste the front and back together.

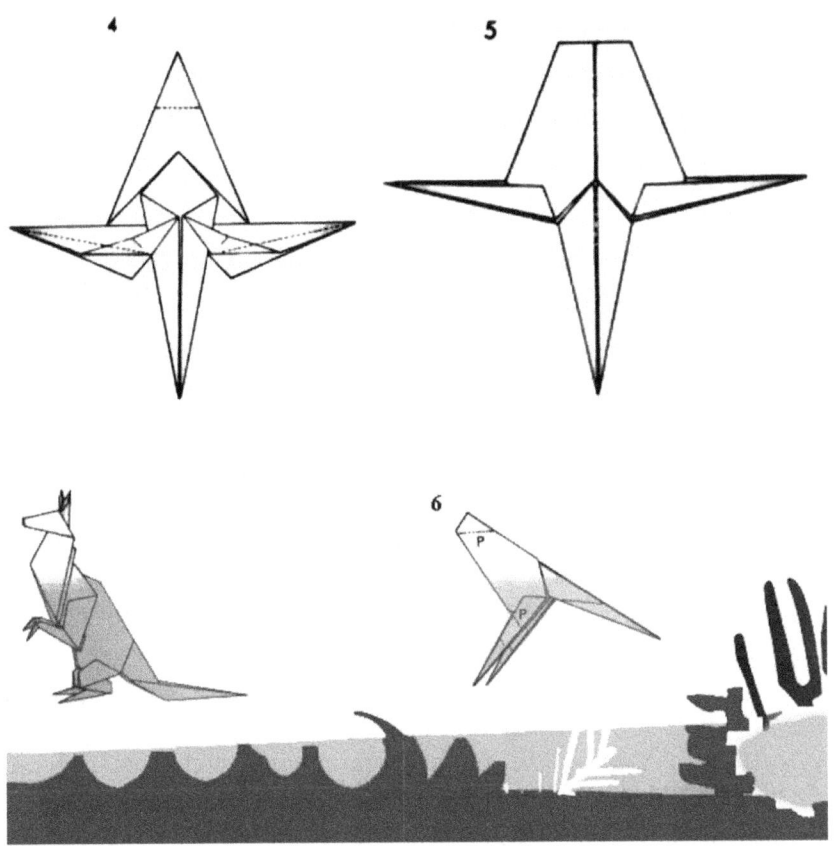

Lobster

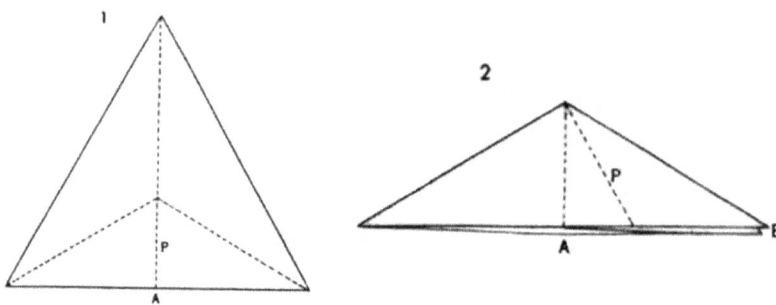

To make this and the wild goose on the next pages, you must cut a piece of paper to make an equilateral triangle, (see General Directions). If you make the lobster with a small sheet of paper, it will look like a shrimp, but if you use a large sheet, it will look like a real lobster.

First crease the paper in half in all three directions. Then in Step 1, lift Point A and fold It in between the other two sides. In Step 2, lift the upper triangle at point B, and open it so that B comes down as shown in Diagram 3.

Step 3 is a little like Steps 8 and 9 in the Basic form. Lift Point B and turn it toward the top. The outer edges will turn inward. Flatten them down along the center line, and crease. Now turn the paper over and repeat Steps 2 and 3 on the other two sides. This will give you the form in 5. In Step 5, turn the flap marked with the arrow over as you would a page in a book. Then, in Step 6, bring Points A and B to the bottom, turning the points outside at the same time.

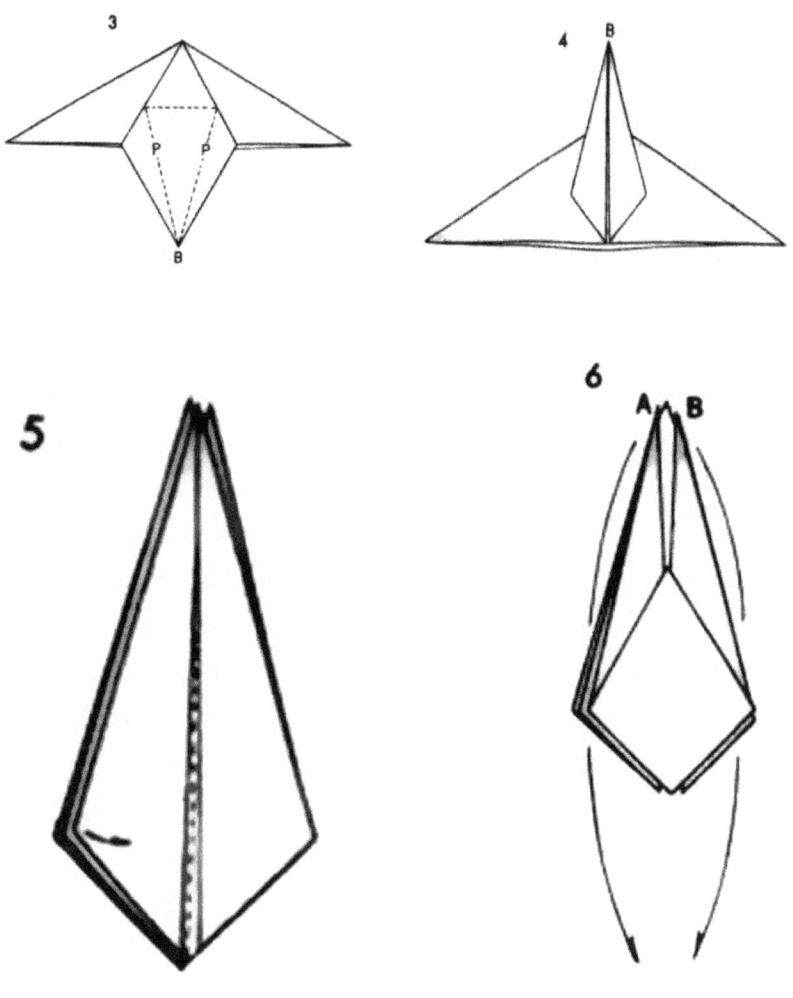

In Step 7 fold the bottom points outside in and up, so that they end up pointing outward. Then in Step 8, fold the points at the head and on the back under. Now fold the body under and over several times. Also fold the outside points all the way over so that they point forward.

In Step 9, fold down the center, and in Step 10, cut slits in the front points and fold back one tip of each to make the lobster's scissors.

Then, holding the body firmly, work each fold in the back out a little so that the tail curves downward.

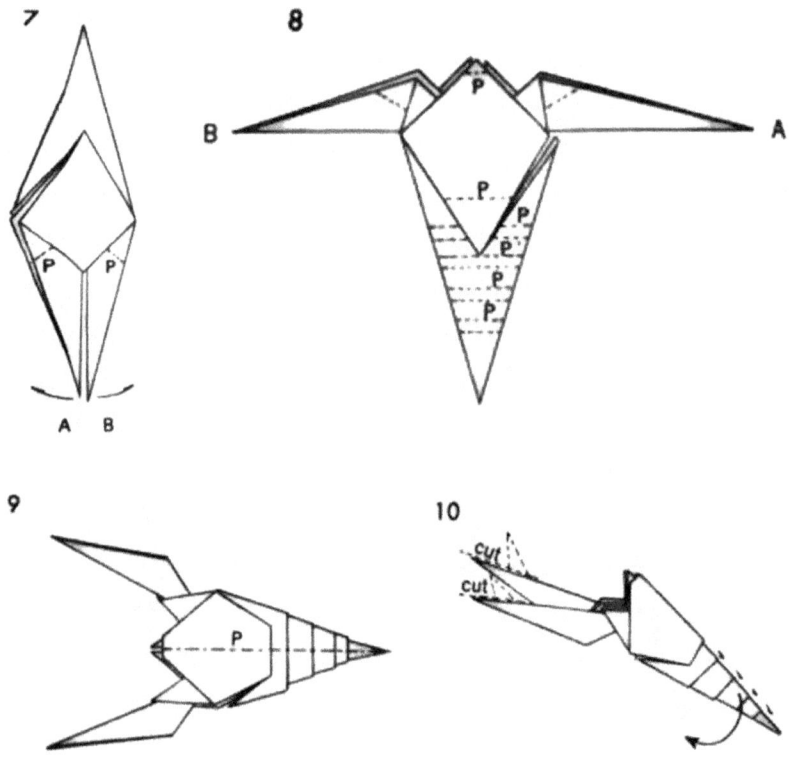

11

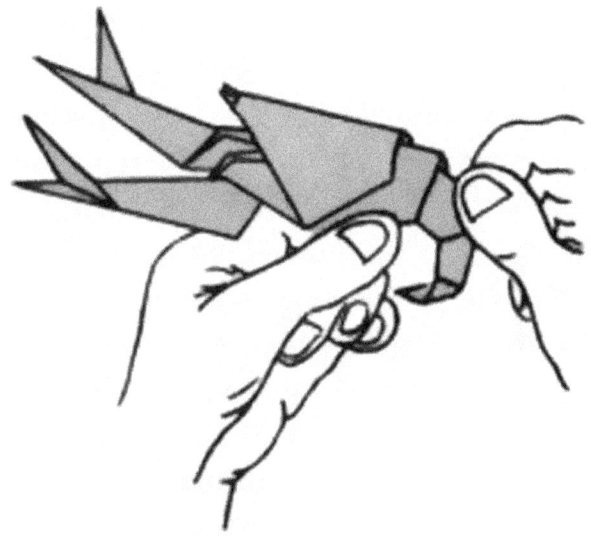

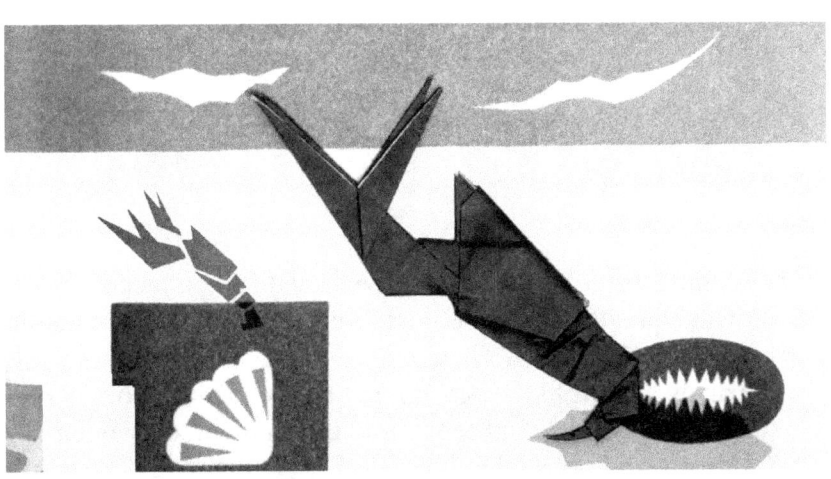

Wild goose

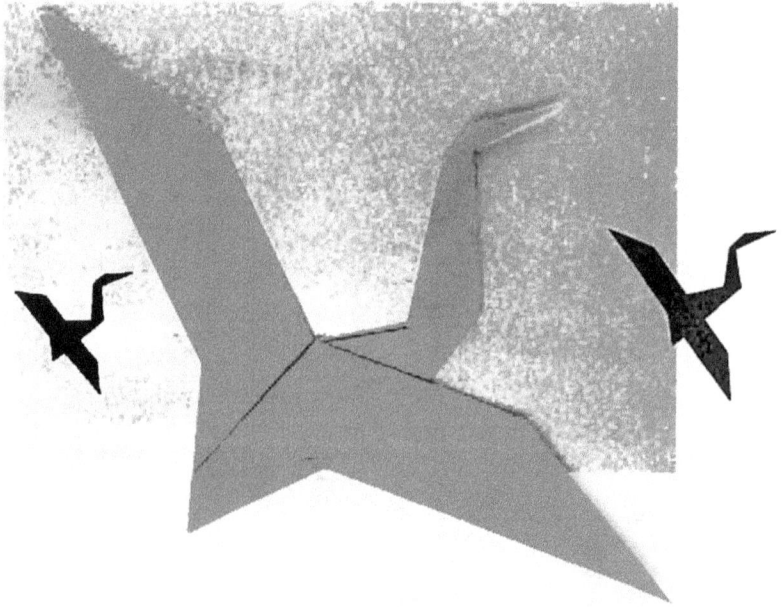

Like the lobster, the wild goose is folded from a piece of paper cut into an equilateral triangle. First crease the paper down the middle in all three directions. Then in Step 1, lift up at the point shown by the arrow, and fold the bottom part so that it comes out between the other two sides. In Step 2, fold the end with only one point inside out and up, so that it now comes out between the two sides and points straight up. This step is just like many you have made in folding birds. In Step 3, open out on both

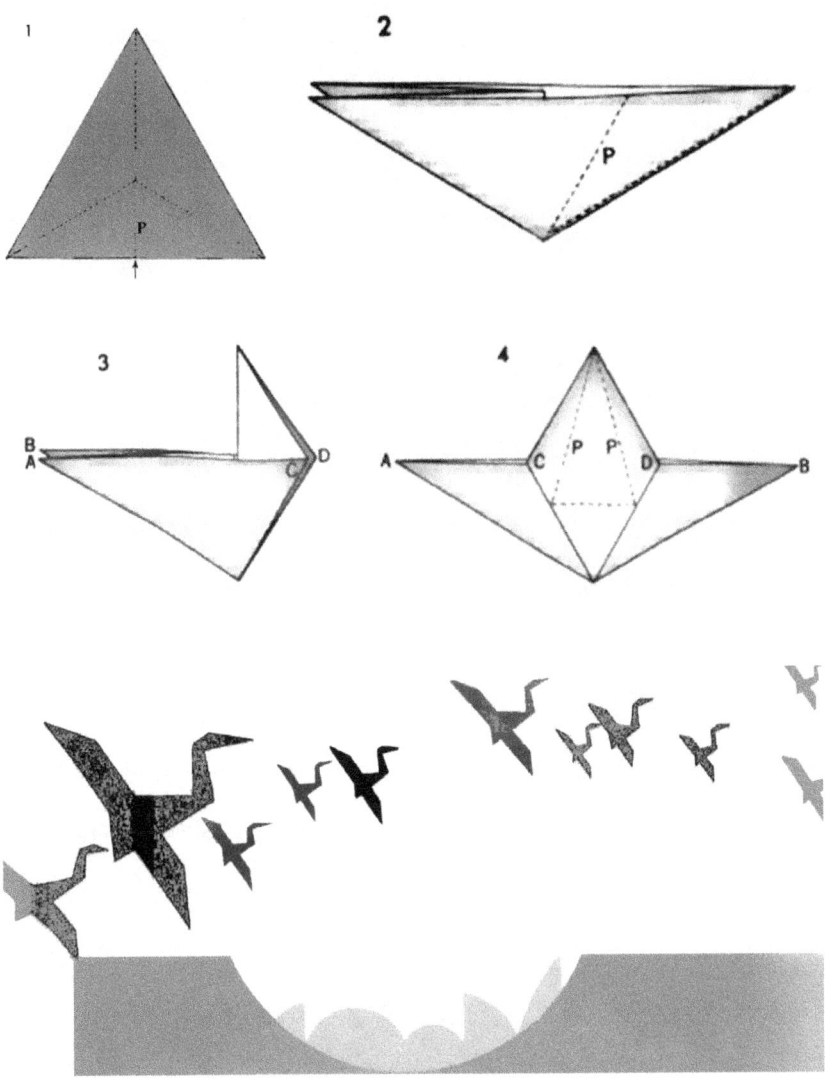

sides so that Points A, B, C, and D come out in the positions shown in 4. Step 4 is a little like Steps 8 and 9 in the basic form. Bring the top point over toward the bottom, and at the same time turn the edges in. in Step 5, fold the point underneath under, so that it now sticks out a little at the top.

Then in Step 6, fold down the center. In Step 7, fold inside out and up along Line 1, and then do the opposite along Line 2. Then spread out the wings to form the finished goose.

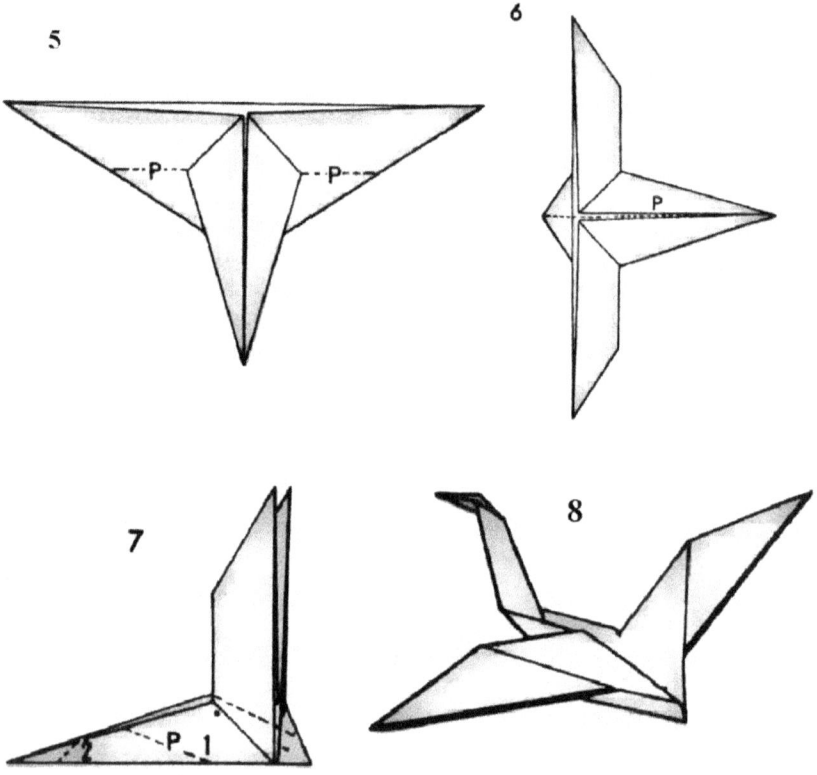

Fox

Head

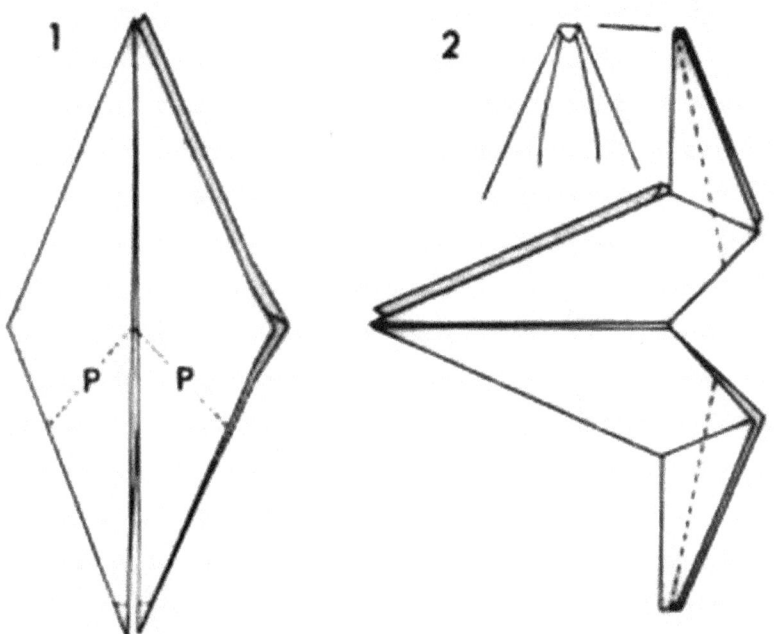

The fox, like the cat, is made in two parts which are then pasted together. Both the head and the tail start from the basic form, and Step 1 is the same for both. In Step 1, fold the lower points so that they point straight out, turning them inside out at the same time.

In Step 2, for the front half, fold the tips of the outer points in, and then fold over on the dotted lines. Turn the paper over, and fold the other side in the same way. In Step 3, fold down the center, and in Step 4, fold the front part back, turning it outside in at the same time.

In Step 5, fold the front layer of the top part forward. Then in Step 6, fold the front point under to make the mouth

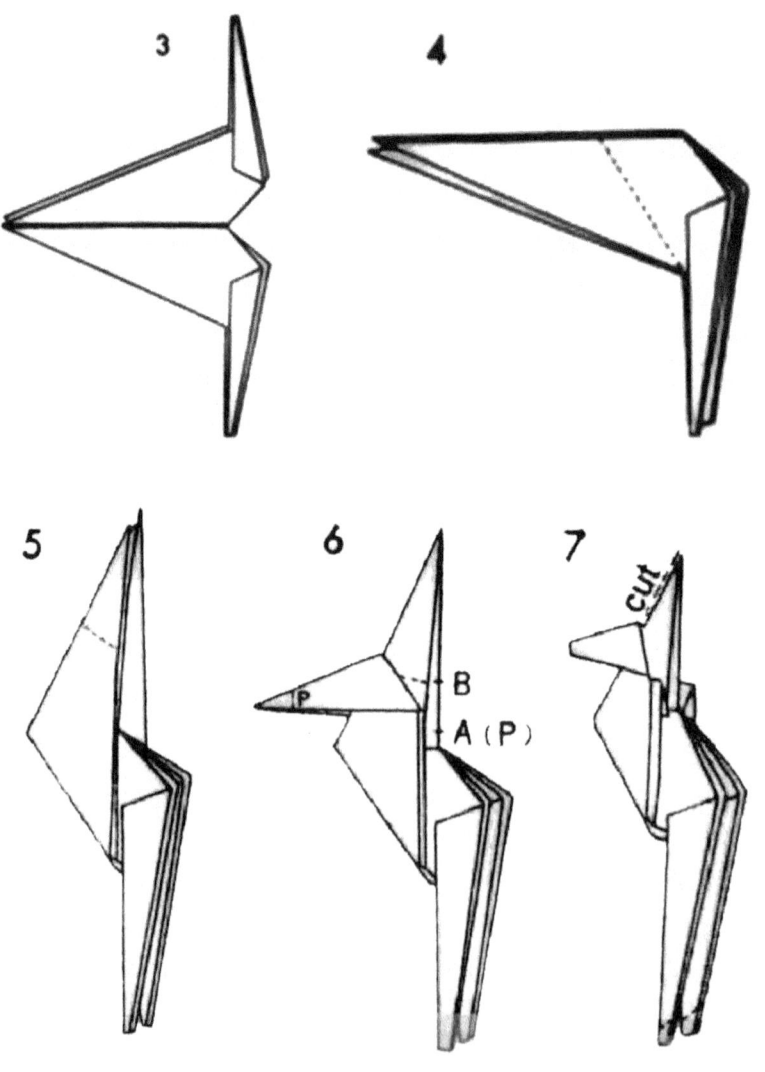

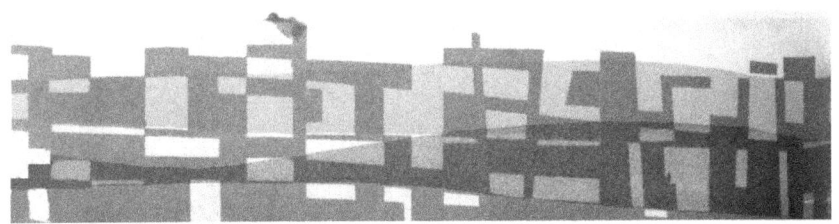

the right shape, and make folds at A and B to lower the ears to the proper height. In Step 7, cut down the center of the top point to separate the ears.

Tail

In Step 2, for the hind part, fold the front flap over. Then in Step 3, fold the inner side points all the way to the center. When you fold Point C over, an edge underneath will stand up. Fold this over and crease so that Point C will go all the way to the center. Do the same with Point D. In Step 4, fold down the center, and In Step 5, put the finishing touches on the tail and legs. Also turn the front point under. In Step 6, fold the front peak inward again to make the curve of the back, and then paste the hind part to the front.

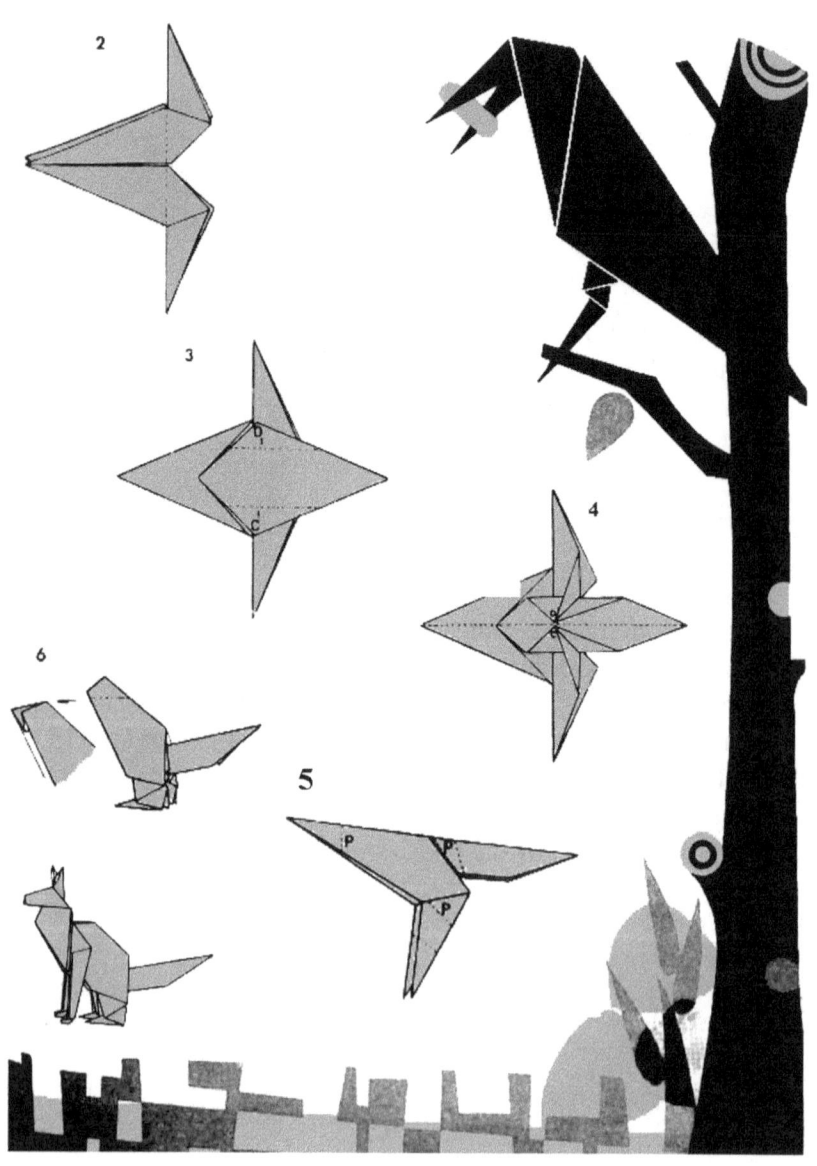

Crow

Start again with the basic form. In Step 1, fold the bottom points out, turning them inside out at the same time. In Step 2. fold the back flap down. Then in Step 3, fold the upper halves of the two small triangles over, and in Steps 4 and 5, refold them as shown. This will make the legs thinner. In Step 6, fold down the center, and in Step 7, make the final folds to form the head and legs.

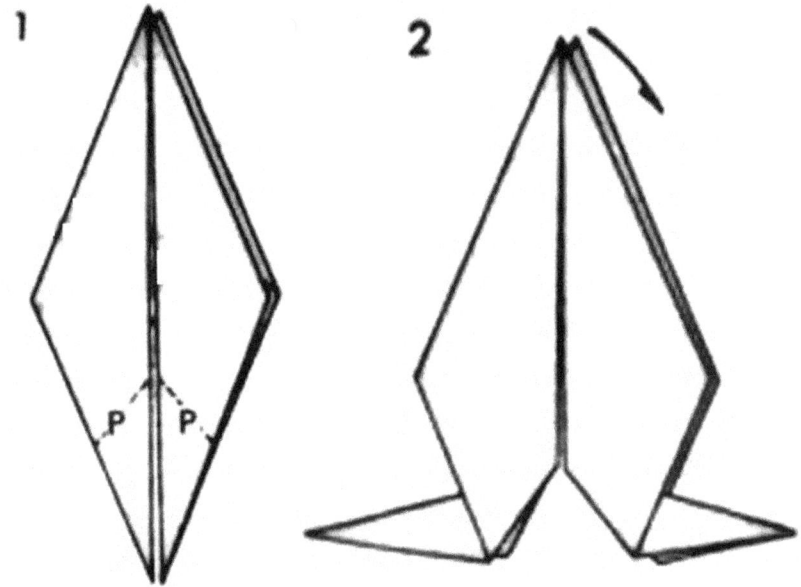

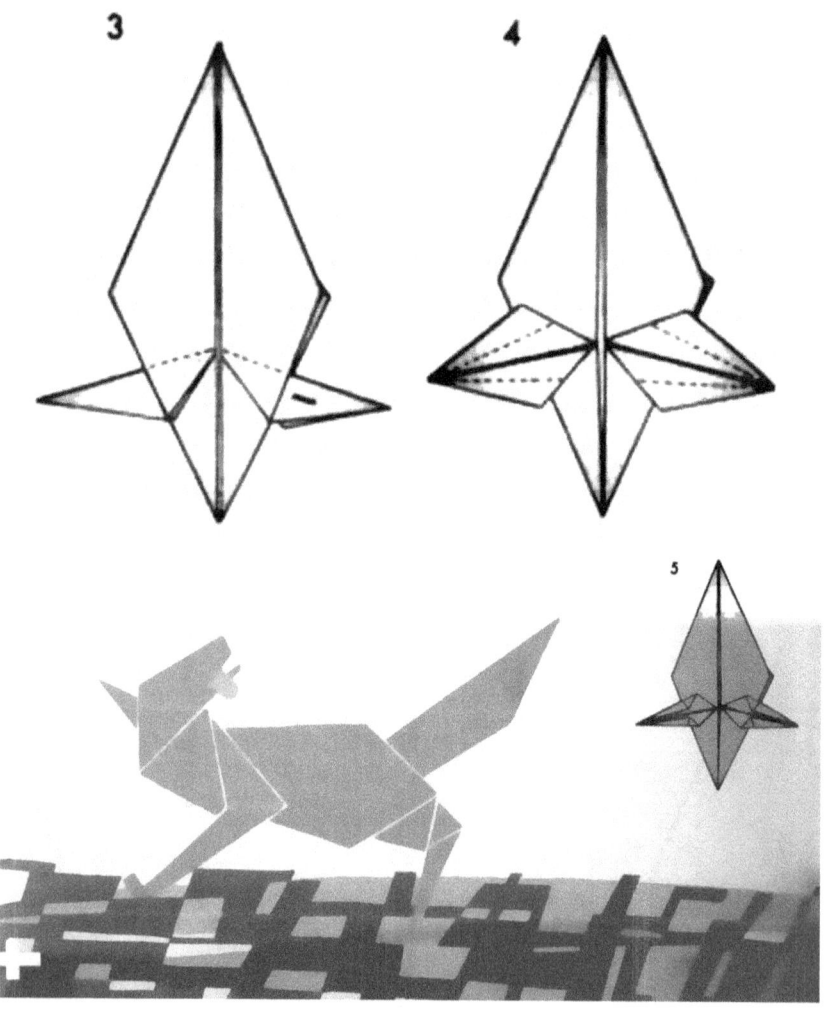

THE FOX AND THE CROW

Once upon a time a crow found a piece of cheese and flew off with it to a tree. She perched on a branch and began to eat the cheese.

Just then a fox came along. He saw the crow, and he saw the cheese. He was hungry and wanted the cheese for his dinner.

" Hello, Mrs. Crow," said the fox. " What a beautiful coat of black feathers you have! Your voice must be as beautiful as your feathers. I'd

56

like to hear you sing a song. If you will sing just one song for me, I will call you the Queen of the Birds."

Mrs. Crow was terribly pleased, and she began to caw and caw. The cheese fell to the ground, and the fox snapped it up and ran. He did not even stop to hear the end of Mrs. Crow's song.

Mrs. Crow squawked with surprise, but there was nothing she could do to get the cheese back.

Always beware of flatterers.

----Aesop's Fables

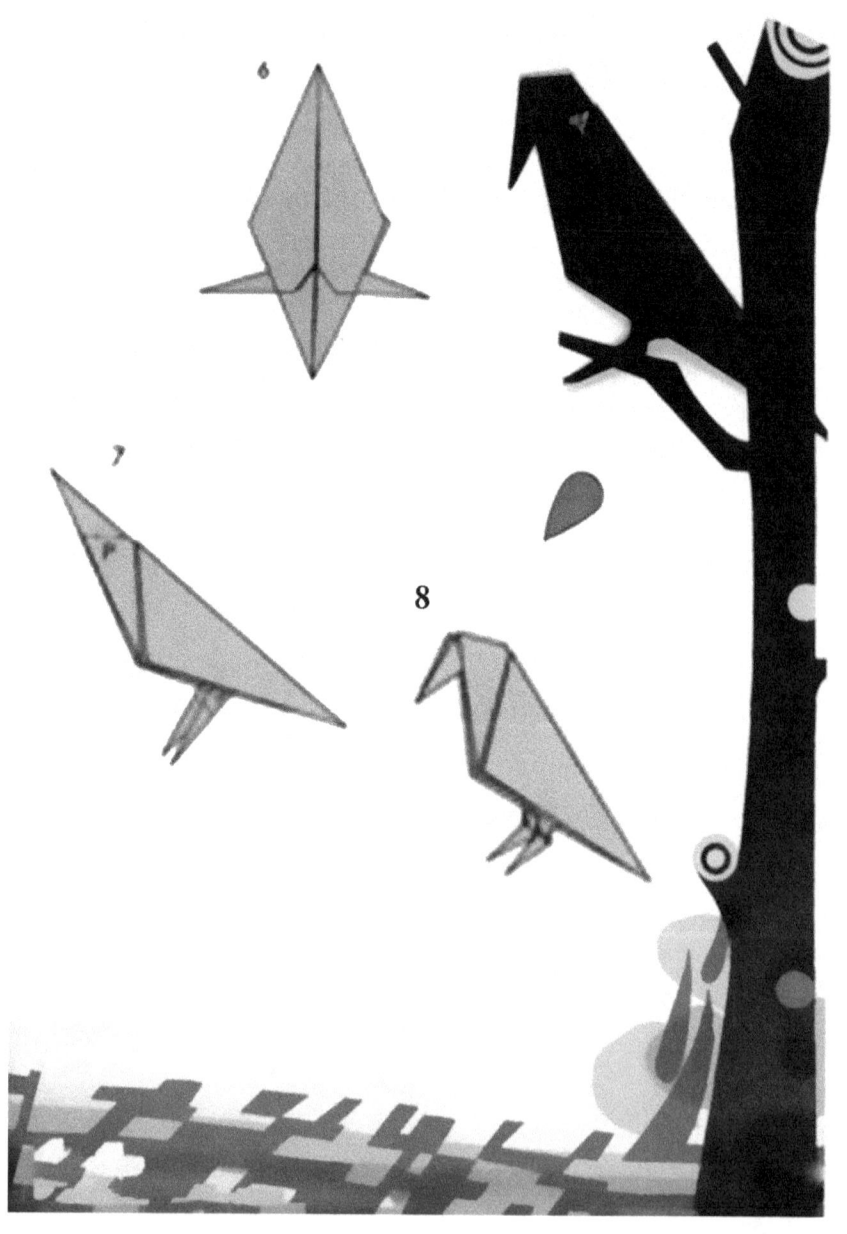